1 How to Buy a House Without a Mortgage: Creative Financing Strategies

Unlocking Alternative Paths to H
Burden of

Idea and Theme:

The core idea of this book is to provide readers with an alternative approach to homeownership by exploring and implementing creative financing strategies that do not rely on traditional mortgage loans. It seeks to challenge the conventional narrative that purchasing a home always requires a large down payment and years of monthly payments to a bank or lender. Instead, it focuses on providing readers with innovative and accessible ways to buy a home without being burdened by debt, which often traps homeowners for decades.

Main Theme:

The theme revolves around **financial freedom** and **empowerment** through **creative financing** methods. The book highlights various non-traditional routes to purchasing a home, emphasizing the potential to build a debt-free future while still achieving the dream of homeownership. The overall message is about **breaking free** from the constraints of traditional financial systems, allowing for flexibility, creativity, and new opportunities in the real estate market.

Target Audience:

This book is intended for individuals who are:

- **Frustrated** with the idea of taking on a 30-year mortgage or those who are looking to avoid the long-term debt cycle.
- **First-time homebuyers**, especially those who may struggle with the high costs of traditional homeownership.
- **Real estate investors** looking for alternative methods of financing.
- People interested in achieving **financial independence** and those seeking **non-traditional wealth-building strategies**.

2   How to Buy a House Without a Mortgage: Creative Financing Strategies

Key Concepts:

1. **Creative Financing**: The book introduces the reader to a range of alternative financing methods, such as seller financing, rent-to-own options, peer-to-peer lending, and bartering, providing step-by-step guidance on how to use them effectively.
2. **Debt-Free Homeownership**: It focuses on strategies that allow buyers to avoid mortgages, thus preventing the long-term financial strain that comes with interest payments and the risk of foreclosure.
3. **Empowerment Through Knowledge**: The book aims to empower readers by educating them on how the traditional mortgage system works, why it may not be the best option for everyone, and how to find creative, viable solutions to secure a home without relying on banks.
4. **Financial Freedom**: By buying a house without a mortgage, readers can significantly reduce their long-term financial obligations, ultimately giving them the freedom to focus on other wealth-building opportunities, investments, or financial goals.
5. **Long-Term Financial Planning**: The book doesn't just teach how to buy a home without a mortgage but also offers advice on how to use these methods to create a sustainable and robust financial future.

Tone:

The tone of the book is **educational yet accessible**, providing clear, actionable advice while breaking down complex financial concepts. It will also be **inspiring**—empowering readers to rethink the conventional path to homeownership and encouraging them to be open to new possibilities.

Theme Exploration:

3 How to Buy a House Without a Mortgage: Creative Financing Strategies

- **Breaking Financial Chains**: Traditional homebuying can feel like an insurmountable challenge, especially with rising home prices and inflation. The book explores how creative financing strategies can provide an escape from these financial chains and allow individuals to own property without the burden of debt.
- **Building Wealth Outside of the Traditional System**: Through real-world examples and actionable steps, the book emphasizes how creative financing strategies can be used not only for homeownership but also as tools for building wealth in the real estate market.
- **Revolutionizing Real Estate**: The book encourages readers to approach homeownership as an evolving, adaptive process, rather than being confined to a rigid, traditional structure. It stresses the importance of adapting to the modern financial landscape, where flexibility and alternative financing are becoming increasingly popular.

Goal:

The goal of this book is to equip readers with a toolkit of alternative financing strategies and to inspire them to take control of their financial futures. By the end of the book, readers will not only have an understanding of how to buy a home without a mortgage but also feel empowered to explore other creative financial paths that can lead them to long-term success and independence.

How to Buy a House Without a Mortgage: Creative Financing Strategies

Chapter 1: Introduction to Buying a Home Without a Mortgage

Subsections:

- The Burden of Traditional Mortgages
- The Growing Popularity of Creative Financing
- Overview of the Book's Strategies

Chapter 2: Understanding the Basics of Creative Financing

Subsections:

- What is Creative Financing?
- The Advantages and Disadvantages of Alternative Financing
- The Legal and Financial Implications

Chapter 3: Exploring Rent-to-Own Options

Subsections:

- How Rent-to-Own Works
- Advantages of Rent-to-Own for Buyers
- How to Structure a Rent-to-Own Agreement
- Negotiating Terms for Success

Chapter 4: Seller Financing: A Debt-Free Alternative

Subsections:

- What is Seller Financing?

5 How to Buy a House Without a Mortgage: Creative Financing Strategies

- How Seller Financing Can Benefit Both Buyers and Sellers
- Crafting a Seller Financing Agreement
- Key Considerations and Negotiation Tips

Chapter 5: Assumption of Mortgage

Subsections:

- What is a Mortgage Assumption?
- When Assumption Makes Sense
- Legal Considerations and Pitfalls
- How to Find Homes with Assumable Mortgages

Chapter 6: Lease Options and Lease Purchase Agreements

Subsections:

- What is a Lease Option?
- How to Structure a Lease Purchase Agreement
- Key Differences Between Rent-to-Own and Lease Options
- Pros and Cons for Buyers

Chapter 7: Using Home Equity for Financing

Subsections:

- Understanding Home Equity
- How to Use Home Equity for a New Home Purchase
- Equity Sharing Agreements
- Risks and Rewards of Equity-Based Financing

6 How to Buy a House Without a Mortgage: Creative Financing Strategies

Chapter 8: Crowdfunding Your Home Purchase

Subsections:

- How Crowdfunding for Real Estate Works
- Setting Up a Real Estate Crowdfunding Campaign
- Legal Aspects of Crowdfunding
- Successful Case Studies of Crowdfunding for Homeownership

Chapter 9: Bartering and Alternative Exchanges

Subsections:

- The Concept of Bartering in Real Estate
- How to Structure a Property Barter Agreement
- Finding Opportunities to Barter for Property
- The Legal and Tax Implications of Bartering Real Estate

Chapter 10: Peer-to-Peer Lending and Private Loans

Subsections:

- How Peer-to-Peer Lending Works for Homebuyers
- Finding the Right Private Lenders
- Loan Structures and Terms for Property Financing
- Assessing Risks and Protecting Your Investment

How to Buy a House Without a Mortgage: Creative Financing Strategies

Chapter 11: Home Seller Donations and Gifts

Subsections:

- Understanding Seller Gifts or Donations
- Legal Considerations for Seller Contributions
- How to Negotiate a Seller Donation for Your Home
- Examples of Successful Home Purchases with Seller Donations

---

Chapter 12: Using Retirement Savings for Home Purchase

Subsections:

- Tapping into Your Retirement Accounts
- Rules and Regulations on Using 401(k)s or IRAs for Real Estate
- Pros and Cons of Using Retirement Savings
- How to Minimize Penalties and Maximize Benefits

Chapter 13: Sweat Equity and Building Your Home

Subsections:

- What is Sweat Equity?
- How to Build Equity Through Home Renovation
- Contracting and DIY Homebuilding
- How Sweat Equity Affects Property Value

Chapter 14: Government and Non-Profit Financing Programs

8   How to Buy a House Without a Mortgage: Creative Financing Strategies

Subsections:

- Available Government Programs for First-Time Homebuyers
- Non-Profit Organizations Supporting Debt-Free Homeownership
- Navigating Financial Assistance and Subsidies
- How to Apply and Qualify for Government-Backed Programs

Chapter 15: Borrowing From Family and Friends

Subsections:

- Structuring a Loan Agreement with Friends or Family
- The Dos and Don'ts of Borrowing from Loved Ones
- How to Ensure a Healthy Financial Relationship
- Repayment Plans and Legal Considerations

Chapter 16: Purchasing a Property with a Business Partner

Subsections:

- Co-Ownership and Business Partnerships for Home Purchase
- Drawing Up a Legal Partnership Agreement
- Managing Shared Ownership of Real Estate
- Exit Strategies and Protection for Co-Owners

Chapter 17: The Art of Negotiation: Getting the Best Deal

9 How to Buy a House Without a Mortgage: Creative Financing Strategies

Subsections:

- Negotiating Without a Traditional Mortgage
- Creative Techniques for Securing the Best Price
- How to Overcome Seller Hesitations
- Using Leverage and Knowledge to Your Advantage

Chapter 18: Building a Network for Creative Financing

Subsections:

- Building a Team of Professionals (Real Estate Agents, Lawyers, etc.)
- Networking for Off-Market Property Deals
- Finding the Right Lenders and Investors
- Joining Communities of Creative Financers

Chapter 19: Closing the Deal: What You Need to Know

Subsections:

- Steps to Finalize a Non-Traditional Home Purchase
- Legal Documents and Paperwork Required
- How to Protect Yourself During Closing
- What to Do After the Deal is Done

Chapter 20: Moving into Your Debt-Free Home

Subsections:

10 **How to Buy a House Without a Mortgage: Creative Financing Strategies**

- How to Transition from Renting or Saving to Owning
- Budgeting for Homeownership Without a Mortgage
- Long-Term Financial Planning After a Non-Traditional Purchase
- Celebrating Your Debt-Free Homeownership Journey

Chapter 21: Building Financial Freedom Through Real Estate

Subsections:

- Creating Long-Term Wealth Through Creative Real Estate Financing
- How to Leverage Your Home as an Asset
- Real Estate Investment Strategies for Future Growth
- Continuing the Journey Toward Financial Independence

Chapter 22: Overcoming Common Obstacles

Subsections:

- Addressing Common Fears and Misconceptions About Debt-Free Homeownership
- How to Handle Rejections or Challenges in the Creative Financing Process
- Dealing with Market Fluctuations and Risk Management
- How to Adapt Your Strategy for Success

Chapter 23: How to Protect Your Home and Investments

Subsections:

11   How to Buy a House Without a Mortgage: Creative Financing Strategies

- Property Insurance and Legal Protection for Non-Traditional Home Buyers
- Structuring Contracts to Avoid Disputes
- Long-Term Maintenance and Financial Care for Your Property
- Estate Planning and Protecting Your Debt-Free Asset

Chapter 24: Future Trends in Creative Financing

Subsections:

- The Future of Homeownership Without Mortgages
- Emerging Trends in Real Estate Financing
- How Technology Is Changing the Creative Financing Landscape
- What to Expect in the Next Decade

Conclusion: Unlocking a Debt-Free Future

Subsections:

- Reflecting on Your Journey to Homeownership
- The Benefits of Living Without a Mortgage
- Final Tips for Continued Success in Real Estate and Financial Freedom
- Taking Action: The Next Steps Toward Your Dream Home

12 How to Buy a House Without a Mortgage: Creative Financing Strategies

Chapter 1: Introduction to Buying a Home Without a Mortgage

In this opening chapter, we will introduce readers to the concept of purchasing a home without relying on a traditional mortgage. We will cover the drawbacks of conventional mortgage systems, explore the increasing shift towards creative financing methods, and provide an overview of the strategies the book will delve into, guiding readers toward debt-free homeownership.

Subsection 1: The Burden of Traditional Mortgages

1.1 Overview of Traditional Mortgages
Traditional home loans, commonly known as mortgages, are often the primary method of financing home purchases. Typically, buyers make a down payment (usually between 5% to 20%) and then repay the rest of the loan amount over a fixed period, typically 30 years. The payments consist of both principal and interest, and the interest is paid over time, significantly increasing the total cost of the home.

1.2 The Financial Strain of Mortgages
While mortgages make homeownership accessible, they come with a significant financial burden. High monthly payments, long repayment terms, and substantial interest rates often cause individuals to be financially tied to the mortgage lender for decades. For many, the mortgage is a long-term financial commitment that consumes a large portion of their income, making it harder to achieve other financial goals, such as saving for retirement, investing, or paying off debt.

1.3 The Psychological and Emotional Toll
The stress of managing a large mortgage can also have psychological effects. The constant worry about making timely payments and the fear of foreclosure can detract from the joy of homeownership. This emotional toll is compounded by the inability to quickly move, downsize, or relocate without incurring heavy financial penalties, such as early mortgage repayment fees or capital gains tax.

13 How to Buy a House Without a Mortgage: Creative Financing Strategies

1.4 The Risk of Debt
Another issue with traditional mortgages is the potential for debt. Homebuyers who rely on loans may find themselves paying for their home long after it is paid off due to the cumulative cost of interest. In extreme cases, when market conditions change, homeowners may also risk negative equity (owing more than their home is worth) or foreclosure if they cannot make payments.

Subsection 2: The Growing Popularity of Creative Financing

2.1 The Shift Toward Alternative Financing
In recent years, homebuyers have begun exploring alternatives to traditional mortgages, driven by the desire to break free from long-term debt. With the growing demand for financial flexibility, the market for creative financing options has expanded. These alternative methods offer various ways to secure homeownership without the burden of a mortgage, from seller financing to lease options, crowdfunding, and more.

2.2 Why Creative Financing is Gaining Popularity
Creative financing is becoming increasingly popular because it provides buyers with more control over the purchasing process and the terms of the agreement. These methods often allow buyers to bypass traditional lenders, offering lower costs, more flexible terms, and opportunities to avoid the burdens of interest and high monthly payments. Moreover, alternative financing can be more accessible to people who might not qualify for a traditional mortgage due to poor credit scores, lack of a substantial down payment, or unconventional employment history.

2.3 Types of Creative Financing
Creative financing encompasses a wide range of strategies, including:

- **Seller Financing**: The seller acts as the lender, and the buyer repays the seller directly instead of a bank.

- **Lease Option (Rent-to-Own)**: The buyer rents the home with an option to purchase it later, often at a predetermined price.
- **House Hacking**: Buying a multi-unit property and renting out units to cover mortgage costs, or buying a property with a separate living space that can be rented out.
- **Peer-to-Peer Lending**: Securing a loan from individual investors through online platforms rather than a bank.
- **Crowdfunding**: Pooling money from multiple investors to finance the purchase of a property.
- **Barter**: In some cases, buyers can use non-monetary exchanges (e.g., services or goods) to help purchase a home.

2.4 The Appeal of Debt-Free Homeownership

Creative financing options make it possible to own a home outright or with a minimal amount of debt, freeing individuals from the long-term financial commitments of a traditional mortgage. By eliminating or reducing interest payments, buyers can allocate their resources more efficiently and focus on building wealth in other areas. Furthermore, these strategies allow for more flexibility in terms of repayment schedules, avoiding the rigid, one-size-fits-all structure of traditional mortgage loans.

2.5 The Role of Technology and Innovation

Advancements in technology have made it easier to explore and implement creative financing strategies. Online platforms, crowdfunding sites, and peer-to-peer lending networks have made it possible for buyers to connect with sellers and investors directly, often without the need for intermediaries like real estate agents or banks. These technological innovations are reshaping the way homeownership is achieved, making it more accessible to a broader range of people.

Subsection 3: Overview of the Book's Strategies

15 How to Buy a House Without a Mortgage: Creative Financing Strategies

3.1 Unlocking Alternative Paths to Homeownership
This book serves as a comprehensive guide to exploring and utilizing creative financing methods to purchase a home. It covers the full spectrum of strategies available, providing readers with a variety of tools to choose from, depending on their unique financial situation and preferences.

3.2 Step-by-Step Guidance
Each chapter of the book will detail specific creative financing strategies, breaking down the key steps involved, the potential risks, and the benefits of each method. The reader will be guided through the process of understanding and applying these strategies to their own homebuying journey. With each strategy, we will provide examples, case studies, and expert advice to help readers assess which methods best align with their goals.

3.3 Understanding the Legal and Financial Landscape
While creative financing can be highly effective, it is important for readers to understand the legal and financial implications of these strategies. This book will provide essential information on the laws and regulations governing alternative financing methods, as well as tips on how to protect oneself from potential pitfalls. In particular, it will cover the importance of conducting due diligence and seeking legal or financial advice before entering into agreements.

3.4 Case Studies and Real-Life Examples
Throughout the book, we will showcase real-life case studies and examples of individuals who have successfully used creative financing strategies to purchase homes. These stories will serve to inspire and motivate readers, illustrating that homeownership without a mortgage is not only possible but also attainable with the right knowledge and resources.

3.5 Key Takeaways
At the end of each chapter, we will summarize the key points and lessons learned, ensuring readers have a clear understanding of how to implement each strategy. The goal is to empower readers with

practical knowledge they can use immediately to begin their journey toward debt-free homeownership.

3.6 Expanding Financial Horizons
The book not only focuses on homeownership but also introduces readers to broader financial concepts and wealth-building strategies that can complement alternative homebuying methods. By the end of the book, readers will have a roadmap for achieving financial freedom, reducing debt, and using creative financing to unlock new opportunities for building wealth.

In conclusion, this chapter introduces the concept of buying a home without a mortgage by highlighting the limitations of traditional mortgage systems, the growing popularity of creative financing, and the strategies explored in the book. The aim is to inspire readers to take a proactive approach to homeownership and financial freedom, equipped with the knowledge and tools to bypass the traditional mortgage system and pursue debt-free paths to homeownership

17 How to Buy a House Without a Mortgage: Creative Financing Strategies

Chapter 2: Understanding the Basics of Creative Financing

In this chapter, we will delve deep into the concept of creative financing, exploring what it is, how it works, and its key advantages and disadvantages. We will also explore the legal and financial implications of utilizing these strategies, equipping the reader with the foundational knowledge needed to pursue homeownership through alternative means. This chapter will set the stage for further exploration of specific creative financing strategies in subsequent chapters.

Subsection 1: What is Creative Financing?

1.1 Definition of Creative Financing
Creative financing refers to alternative methods of funding a property purchase that differ from the traditional mortgage route. Unlike conventional home loans, where a buyer typically borrows money from a bank or financial institution to purchase a home, creative financing involves various non-traditional methods that provide greater flexibility and can bypass the need for banks or mortgage lenders altogether. Creative financing strategies allow buyers to structure deals in ways that suit both their financial situation and the seller's needs, often with more favorable terms.

1.2 Key Features of Creative Financing
Creative financing is characterized by several features that make it distinct from traditional mortgage methods:

- **Non-Traditional Lenders**: Buyers may work directly with the seller or other private lenders, such as peer-to-peer platforms, instead of relying on a bank.
- **Flexible Terms**: Buyers and sellers have the freedom to negotiate terms such as the interest rate, repayment schedule, and down payment, allowing for more personalized agreements.

- **Low or No Interest**: Some creative financing options involve little or no interest payments, which can make the overall cost of the home much more affordable over time.
- **Debt-Free Options**: Creative financing strategies may allow buyers to purchase a home outright or with minimal debt, avoiding the burden of a traditional mortgage.

1.3 Types of Creative Financing Methods
Creative financing encompasses a variety of strategies, including but not limited to:

- **Seller Financing**: The seller acts as the lender and allows the buyer to make payments directly to them instead of going through a bank.
- **Lease Options (Rent-to-Own)**: Buyers rent the property with the option to purchase it later, often with part of the rent going toward the purchase price.
- **Subject-To Financing**: The buyer takes control of the seller's existing mortgage payments without formally assuming the loan.
- **Equity Sharing**: The buyer and a co-investor (such as a family member or a friend) share ownership of the property, with the buyer living in the property and paying the mortgage.
- **Seller Carryback**: A seller agrees to "carry back" part of the loan, meaning they provide a portion of the financing while the buyer secures the rest from another source.

1.4 How Creative Financing Works
The essence of creative financing lies in its flexibility. Instead of following the rigid structure of a traditional mortgage, creative financing allows for negotiations and tailoring of terms to suit the unique needs of the buyer and the seller. This flexibility makes creative financing particularly appealing in situations where traditional loans may not be an option, such as in the case of buyers with poor credit, self-employed individuals, or those who do not have a large down payment.

19 How to Buy a House Without a Mortgage: Creative Financing Strategies

Subsection 2: The Advantages and Disadvantages of Alternative Financing

2.1 Advantages of Creative Financing

Creative financing offers numerous benefits to homebuyers, including:

- **Lower Costs**: By bypassing banks and traditional lenders, homebuyers can avoid hefty closing costs, loan fees, and sometimes, even interest. In some cases, creative financing methods, like seller financing, can offer little or no interest on the loan.
- **Flexibility in Terms**: Creative financing gives both buyers and sellers the flexibility to negotiate terms that fit their specific situations, such as the length of repayment, interest rates, or down payments.
- **No Traditional Credit Checks**: Since creative financing typically does not involve banks, buyers may avoid the strict credit requirements often associated with mortgages. This is especially beneficial for those with less-than-perfect credit.
- **Faster Process**: Traditional mortgage approval can be time-consuming, often taking weeks or months. Creative financing strategies, such as seller financing or rent-to-own, may expedite the homebuying process.
- **Avoiding Foreclosure**: In some cases, creative financing can be a way for homeowners facing foreclosure to sell their property without the negative consequences that often accompany a bank foreclosure.

2.2 Disadvantages of Creative Financing

Despite the numerous advantages, creative financing methods also come with risks and limitations:

- **Higher Risk for Buyers**: Creative financing often comes with less legal protection compared to traditional mortgages.

If a seller defaults or refuses to honor their agreement, the buyer may have limited recourse.
- **Potentially Higher Interest Rates**: While creative financing can sometimes result in low or no interest rates, other methods may have higher interest rates than traditional loans, particularly in private loans.
- **Difficulty in Finding Sellers**: Not all sellers are open to creative financing, and some may prefer the security and certainty of a traditional sale through a bank.
- **Unconventional Terms**: Since creative financing involves more negotiation, the terms of the deal might be complex and require expert understanding. If buyers do not fully understand the agreement, they may find themselves in an unfavorable position.
- **Limited Availability**: While creative financing is becoming more popular, it is still not as widely used or understood as traditional mortgages. As such, it may be harder to find viable opportunities in certain markets.

Subsection 3: The Legal and Financial Implications

3.1 Legal Considerations in Creative Financing

The legal landscape surrounding creative financing is complex and varies depending on the type of financing used. Buyers and sellers should be aware of the following key legal implications:

- **Written Agreements**: It is crucial to have formal, written contracts when engaging in creative financing, as verbal agreements may not hold up in court. This protects both parties in the event of a dispute.
- **Title Transfer**: With some creative financing methods, such as subject-to financing, it is important to understand how title transfer works. In some cases, the buyer may not immediately assume legal ownership of the property, leading to potential complications.

- **State and Local Laws**: Laws governing alternative financing methods can vary significantly by jurisdiction. It is essential to consult with a real estate attorney or professional familiar with local regulations to ensure compliance.
- **Foreclosure and Default Risks**: In cases like seller financing, if the buyer defaults on the payment, the seller may have the legal right to initiate foreclosure proceedings, even if the buyer has made significant payments. Understanding these legal rights is vital before entering into such agreements.

3.2 Financial Considerations and Tax Implications

Aside from the legal side, creative financing also involves significant financial implications that need careful consideration:

- **Tax Implications**: Buyers should be aware of potential tax implications, such as capital gains taxes when selling a home or the treatment of interest under creative financing methods. Depending on the financing method, the seller may also be required to report the interest income as taxable earnings.
- **Cash Flow Management**: Buyers using creative financing methods must be able to manage their cash flow carefully. Since payments can vary significantly depending on the terms of the agreement, mismanagement could lead to missed payments or financial distress.
- **Long-Term Financial Planning**: While creative financing may offer short-term relief, buyers should consider the long-term financial impact. For example, using rent-to-own strategies may lead to higher overall costs, and some methods may require significant upfront capital or ongoing maintenance costs.

3.3 The Role of Professional Advice

Given the complexities involved in creative financing, it is advisable for buyers and sellers to seek professional advice. Real estate agents, financial advisors, and attorneys can provide valuable guidance to ensure the terms of the deal are fair, legally sound, and financially feasible. Engaging professionals helps prevent potential legal or financial pitfalls and ensures that both parties understand their obligations and rights.

Conclusion

Understanding the basics of creative financing is crucial for anyone interested in purchasing a home without a mortgage. This chapter has provided a thorough overview of what creative financing is, its key advantages and disadvantages, and the legal and financial implications that come with these methods. Armed with this knowledge, readers will be better prepared to explore and implement creative financing strategies in their journey toward debt-free homeownership. The following chapters will explore specific strategies in detail, providing the reader with a practical roadmap for pursuing these alternatives.

23 How to Buy a House Without a Mortgage: Creative Financing Strategies

Chapter 3: Exploring Rent-to-Own Options

Rent-to-own agreements, also known as lease options, have become an increasingly popular method for buyers looking to purchase a home without the need for a traditional mortgage. This chapter will thoroughly explore rent-to-own options, delving into how they work, their advantages for buyers, the process of structuring a rent-to-own agreement, and how to negotiate favorable terms. By the end of this chapter, readers will have a clear understanding of how rent-to-own can be an effective alternative to traditional home buying methods, and the tools needed to make it a viable path to homeownership.

Subsection 1: How Rent-to-Own Works

1.1 Overview of Rent-to-Own Agreements
Rent-to-own is a type of agreement in which a tenant rents a property with the option to purchase it at a later date, usually within a specified period, typically ranging from one to three years. A portion of the monthly rent is often credited toward the eventual down payment or purchase price of the home, which allows tenants to gradually build equity while living in the property. This agreement can be appealing for individuals who may not currently have the necessary funds for a down payment or the credit score to secure a traditional mortgage.

1.2 Structure of Rent-to-Own Agreements
A rent-to-own agreement typically consists of two key components:

- **Lease Agreement**: The buyer rents the property for a specific term at a set monthly rent price. The rent payment is often higher than market rent, with the excess being credited toward the future purchase price or down payment.
- **Option to Purchase**: The agreement includes a clause giving the tenant the exclusive right to purchase the property at a pre-agreed price within the option period. This price is

usually set at the beginning of the lease term, although it may also include an adjustment for market conditions.

1.3 Terms and Conditions
The rent-to-own agreement is legally binding, and both parties must abide by the terms outlined in the contract. While the tenant has the option to purchase the property, they are not obligated to do so. The seller, on the other hand, is required to honor the agreement and not sell the property to anyone else during the option period. Some common elements that are typically outlined in the contract include:

- **Purchase Price**: Often set at the beginning of the lease, though it can be subject to adjustment.
- **Lease Term**: The length of the rental period, usually one to three years.
- **Rent Credit**: A portion of the rent paid each month that is credited toward the purchase price or down payment.
- **Option Fee**: A non-refundable fee paid upfront, typically 1% to 5% of the purchase price, which gives the buyer the option to purchase the property at the end of the lease.

1.4 Legal and Financial Considerations
Rent-to-own agreements can be complex, so it's essential to understand the legal implications. Both parties should ensure the contract is clear about rights, obligations, and timelines. For buyers, it's crucial to review the terms carefully, as they often cannot be easily renegotiated once signed. Likewise, sellers should ensure the agreement is legally enforceable to avoid potential legal disputes later on. Consulting a real estate attorney is highly recommended for both parties to ensure that the terms of the agreement are legally sound.

Subsection 2: Advantages of Rent-to-Own for Buyers

2.1 Building Equity While Renting
One of the main advantages of rent-to-own agreements is the

25 How to Buy a House Without a Mortgage: Creative Financing Strategies

opportunity for renters to build equity in the property while they are still renting. A portion of the monthly rent payments is credited toward the down payment or purchase price, allowing the tenant to effectively save for the home while living in it. This can be a great way for renters to transition into homeownership without needing to secure a large down payment upfront.

2.2 No Need for Immediate Financing

Rent-to-own provides buyers with time to improve their financial situation. This is particularly beneficial for individuals with poor credit or those who may not have enough savings for a down payment. Over the term of the lease, buyers can work on improving their credit score, saving money, and strengthening their financial standing, which may make it easier to secure financing when they are ready to purchase the home.

2.3 Locking in Purchase Price

In many rent-to-own agreements, the purchase price is locked in at the time the lease is signed, which can be a significant benefit if home prices are rising. Buyers are effectively "securing" a home at a potentially lower price than what the market may offer in the future. Even if property values increase during the term of the lease, the buyer can still purchase the property at the agreed-upon price, potentially saving money in the long term.

2.4 Less Competition

Rent-to-own options can also help buyers avoid the highly competitive nature of traditional home buying, especially in a hot housing market. When you buy a home traditionally, you often face competition from other buyers, which can drive up prices. Rent-to-own agreements typically attract fewer buyers, which can make it easier to negotiate better terms.

2.5 Flexibility

Rent-to-own offers buyers the flexibility of not being locked into purchasing the home at the end of the lease. If their financial situation changes or they decide the home is not right for them, they are not obligated to buy the property. This option is particularly appealing to those who may be uncertain about their long-term housing plans or those who may need time to assess the property or neighborhood.

2.6 Time to Test the Home and Neighborhood
Rent-to-own allows buyers to live in the home and get a real feel for the property and the neighborhood before committing to the purchase. This gives them the opportunity to address any potential issues, such as maintenance problems, neighborhood dynamics, or commute times, before fully committing to homeownership.

Subsection 3: How to Structure a Rent-to-Own Agreement

3.1 The Importance of Clear Terms
The key to a successful rent-to-own agreement is clarity. Both parties—buyer and seller—must agree on the specifics of the lease and purchase options. Clear terms help avoid potential disputes later on. Essential details that should be outlined in the agreement include:

- **Rent and Rent Credit**: How much of the monthly rent payment will be credited toward the purchase price.
- **Option Fee**: The upfront, non-refundable fee the buyer will pay to secure the option to purchase.
- **Purchase Price**: The price at which the home will be bought at the end of the lease term.
- **Lease Term**: The length of the lease period, typically one to three years.
- **Maintenance and Repairs**: Clarifying who is responsible for maintenance and repairs during the lease period.

3.2 Setting the Purchase Price
The purchase price should be agreed upon upfront. This is a critical element of the agreement, as it establishes the amount the buyer will pay for the property. The price may be set based on the current

market value or may include an escalation clause that adjusts the price based on the market conditions at the time the lease ends. Buyers and sellers must consider market trends and property appreciation when setting the price.

3.3 Rent Credit Allocation
Rent credits are typically a percentage of the monthly rent payment that is applied toward the purchase price. For example, if the monthly rent is $1,500 and the rent credit is 20%, $300 of each month's rent payment is applied to the down payment. The rent credit can vary depending on the agreement, and it's important for both parties to agree on how it will be calculated and when it will be credited.

3.4 Option Fee and Refundability
The option fee is typically non-refundable and is a form of earnest money. This fee gives the buyer the right to purchase the home at the end of the lease term. While this fee is usually credited toward the purchase price, it is non-refundable if the buyer decides not to purchase the property at the end of the lease term.

Subsection 4: Negotiating Terms for Success

4.1 The Role of Negotiation in Rent-to-Own
Negotiating terms in a rent-to-own agreement is essential to ensuring both parties are satisfied with the arrangement. Buyers should negotiate for favorable terms, such as a lower purchase price, higher rent credits, and more favorable financing options. Sellers, on the other hand, may seek security in the form of a larger option fee or a higher rent payment to mitigate the risk of the buyer defaulting on the agreement.

4.2 Key Points to Negotiate

- **Option Fee**: Buyers can negotiate for a lower option fee, particularly if they have the ability to make higher rent payments.
- **Purchase Price**: Buyers may want to negotiate a purchase price that is below the current market value or one that includes clauses for price adjustments if property values increase during the lease term.
- **Rent Credits**: Negotiating a higher rent credit percentage can help buyers accumulate a larger portion of the down payment.
- **Lease Term**: The lease term should be long enough to allow the buyer to save for a down payment, improve their credit score, or adjust to changes in financial circumstances.

4.3 Seeking Professional Help

Both buyers and sellers should consider hiring professionals such as real estate agents or attorneys to help negotiate the terms of the rent-to-own agreement. These professionals can ensure that the agreement is fair, legally binding, and tailored to the needs of both parties.

Conclusion

Rent-to-own offers a unique and flexible pathway to homeownership for individuals who may not be able to obtain traditional financing. By understanding how these agreements work, their advantages, how to structure them, and how to negotiate favorable terms, potential buyers can position themselves to successfully purchase a home without a mortgage. This chapter has equipped you with the knowledge needed to navigate the rent-to-own process, making it a valuable tool on your journey to homeownership.

29 How to Buy a House Without a Mortgage: Creative Financing Strategies

Chapter 4: Seller Financing: A Debt-Free Alternative

Seller financing, also referred to as owner financing, provides an alternative path to homeownership that avoids traditional mortgage lenders and the associated debt burden. This chapter explores how seller financing works, its benefits for both buyers and sellers, how to craft a seller financing agreement, and key considerations to keep in mind when negotiating these deals. Through a thorough understanding of seller financing, readers can take advantage of a unique way to buy a home without relying on banks or mortgages.

Subsection 1: What is Seller Financing?

1.1 Definition of Seller Financing
Seller financing is a real estate transaction in which the seller acts as the lender, providing the buyer with a loan to purchase the property. Instead of the buyer obtaining a traditional mortgage from a bank or financial institution, the seller directly finances the sale, and the buyer agrees to repay the loan, typically in monthly installments over a specified period. This agreement bypasses the need for a bank or lender entirely.

1.2 How Seller Financing Works
In a seller financing agreement, the buyer and seller agree on the terms of the sale, including the purchase price, interest rate, repayment schedule, and the loan term. Instead of a bank providing funds, the seller agrees to accept a down payment and the remaining balance is paid over time through agreed-upon installment payments. The seller may hold the title to the property until the loan is paid off in full or may transfer it to the buyer with a lien until the loan is settled.

- **Down Payment**: Similar to a traditional mortgage, the buyer typically makes a down payment to the seller at the start of

the agreement. The size of the down payment can vary but often ranges from 5% to 20% of the purchase price.
- **Loan Terms**: The seller and buyer agree on the loan terms, including the interest rate (often higher than traditional mortgages), loan duration (typically 5 to 30 years), and monthly payments.
- **Repayment Structure**: Repayment can be set up in a way that suits both the buyer and seller. Payments may be made monthly, quarterly, or even annually depending on the arrangement, with terms often similar to those of traditional loans.

1.3 Benefits of Seller Financing

Seller financing can be attractive for both buyers and sellers for a variety of reasons. For buyers, it provides a path to homeownership even if they have trouble securing a traditional mortgage. For sellers, it can result in a quicker sale, an opportunity to earn interest income, and the flexibility to set their own terms.

Subsection 2: How Seller Financing Can Benefit Both Buyers and Sellers

2.1 Benefits for Buyers

- **No Bank Approval Required**: One of the primary advantages of seller financing for buyers is that it doesn't require approval from a bank or mortgage lender. Buyers with poor credit, self-employed individuals, or those who have trouble getting a traditional loan may find this option much easier.
- **Flexible Terms**: Seller financing allows for more flexibility in structuring the loan terms. Buyers can often negotiate the interest rate, down payment, and repayment schedule with the seller, tailoring the deal to their financial situation.

How to Buy a House Without a Mortgage: Creative Financing Strategies

- **Lower Closing Costs**: Traditional home loans typically come with various closing costs, including loan origination fees, appraisal fees, and title insurance. With seller financing, these costs can be significantly lower, as there are no third-party lenders involved.
- **Potential for Lower Interest Rates**: Sellers may offer interest rates that are lower than traditional mortgage lenders, particularly if the property is in a hot market or if the buyer has a good relationship with the seller.
- **Faster Process**: Without the lengthy and often complex process of securing bank financing, the homebuying process can be much quicker. Buyers can often move forward with a sale as soon as both parties agree to the terms.

2.2 Benefits for Sellers

- **Faster Sale**: Seller financing can make the property more appealing to a wider pool of potential buyers, especially those who may not qualify for traditional mortgages. This can result in a quicker sale.
- **Higher Sale Price**: In some cases, sellers may be able to command a higher sale price because they are offering an alternative financing option. Buyers who are unable to secure traditional financing might be willing to pay a premium for the opportunity to purchase a property via seller financing.
- **Monthly Income**: By offering seller financing, sellers can generate a consistent stream of income through monthly payments, similar to receiving a rental income, but without the responsibilities of being a landlord.
- **Tax Benefits**: Sellers may be able to defer some of the capital gains taxes through installment sales, as they only pay taxes on the portion of the sale price received each year, rather than paying all of the tax upfront.
- **Interest Income**: In addition to selling the property, the seller can earn interest on the loan over time, which can be especially beneficial in a high-interest-rate environment.

Subsection 3: Crafting a Seller Financing Agreement

3.1 Key Elements of a Seller Financing Agreement

A seller financing agreement should clearly outline the terms and conditions of the sale to avoid future misunderstandings. The agreement typically includes the following key components:

- **Purchase Price**: The agreed-upon price of the property.
- **Down Payment**: The upfront payment made by the buyer to the seller. This is typically a percentage of the purchase price.
- **Loan Amount**: The remaining balance after the down payment is subtracted from the purchase price.
- **Interest Rate**: The rate at which interest will be charged on the loan. This can be negotiated between the buyer and the seller but may be higher than the market rate for traditional mortgages.
- **Repayment Terms**: This includes the length of the loan, the payment schedule (monthly, quarterly, etc.), and the amount of each payment.
- **Amortization Schedule**: The schedule outlining how the loan will be paid down over time, including the breakdown between principal and interest payments.
- **Prepayment Clause**: Whether the buyer can pay off the loan early without penalty or if there is a prepayment penalty.
- **Default and Consequences**: Terms related to the buyer's default on the loan, such as late fees, foreclosure proceedings, or other actions the seller can take if the buyer fails to make payments.
- **Balloon Payment**: If the loan includes a balloon payment, the agreement should specify when and how the final, large payment will be made. A balloon payment is often due at the end of the loan term.

3.2 Legal Considerations

Since seller financing involves private individuals rather than a financial institution, it's crucial to ensure that the agreement is legally sound. Both parties should:

- **Consult Legal Professionals**: To ensure the agreement adheres to state and local laws and is enforceable in court.
- **Title Search**: A thorough title search should be conducted to ensure that the property is free from any legal claims or liens that could complicate the sale.
- **Promissory Note**: The buyer and seller should both sign a legally binding promissory note that outlines the specifics of the loan, including repayment terms and conditions.
- **Deed of Trust or Mortgage**: The seller should also consider using a deed of trust or mortgage to secure the loan, giving them a legal right to reclaim the property if the buyer defaults.

3.3 Closing Process
Once the agreement is structured, the closing process for a seller-financed transaction is typically quicker and simpler than traditional closings. However, buyers and sellers should still ensure that all the necessary documentation is signed and filed appropriately.

Subsection 4: Key Considerations and Negotiation Tips

4.1 Assessing the Risk of Seller Financing
While seller financing offers many benefits, it also involves certain risks, particularly for sellers. The most significant risks include:

- **Buyer's Ability to Repay**: Sellers may be concerned about the buyer defaulting on the loan, which could result in costly legal proceedings or foreclosure.
- **Property Value Fluctuations**: If property values decline, the seller could find themselves in a situation where the loan balance exceeds the value of the property.

- **Legal Issues**: Without proper legal documentation, sellers may face challenges in enforcing the terms of the agreement.

4.2 Negotiating Terms for Success

When negotiating a seller financing deal, both parties should be prepared to discuss and agree on several key elements:

- **Interest Rate**: Buyers should aim to negotiate a competitive interest rate, while sellers may want to set a rate that reflects the risks they are taking on.
- **Down Payment**: Buyers should negotiate a manageable down payment, while sellers may want to ensure that the down payment is substantial enough to protect their investment.
- **Repayment Schedule**: Both parties should negotiate a repayment schedule that fits their financial needs and goals.

4.3 Professional Help and Resources

Both parties should consider seeking professional help when negotiating a seller financing agreement. Real estate attorneys and financial advisors can help ensure that the terms are fair and legally sound. Working with a real estate agent can also help facilitate the process and ensure that the property is properly marketed and valued.

Conclusion

Seller financing is a valuable alternative for both buyers and sellers looking for a flexible and debt-free approach to homeownership. By bypassing traditional mortgage lenders, buyers can take advantage of flexible terms, while sellers can earn interest on the loan and close the sale faster. This chapter has provided a comprehensive guide to understanding seller financing, including its benefits, how to structure an agreement, and key negotiation tips to help you navigate the process successfully.

35   How to Buy a House Without a Mortgage: Creative Financing Strategies

Chapter 5: Assumption of Mortgage

The assumption of mortgage is a creative financing strategy that allows buyers to take over the seller's existing mortgage, rather than obtaining a new one from a bank or lender. This approach can be a viable alternative to traditional home financing, particularly when interest rates are high or when buyers want to avoid the lengthy process of securing a new mortgage. This chapter provides an in-depth exploration of mortgage assumptions, how they work, when they make sense, legal considerations, and how to find homes with assumable mortgages.

Subsection 1: What is a Mortgage Assumption?

1.1 Definition of Mortgage Assumption
A mortgage assumption occurs when a homebuyer takes over the seller's existing mortgage and becomes responsible for the remaining balance of the loan. The buyer essentially steps into the seller's shoes, agreeing to continue making payments under the same terms and conditions as the original borrower. This can be an attractive option for both parties, as it may allow the buyer to take advantage of the seller's existing loan terms, including interest rates and repayment schedules, which may be more favorable than those available through traditional financing options.

1.2 How Mortgage Assumption Works
In a mortgage assumption, the buyer assumes the remaining mortgage debt, and the lender approves the transfer of the loan from the seller to the buyer. There are typically two types of mortgage assumptions: **"assumable"** and **"non-assumable."**

- **Assumable Mortgages**: These mortgages allow the buyer to take over the loan without needing to apply for a new mortgage or go through the usual approval process. Typically,

government-backed loans, such as FHA, VA, and USDA loans, are assumable, subject to lender approval.
- **Non-Assumable Mortgages**: These loans do not allow for the transfer of responsibility. Most conventional loans are non-assumable, meaning the buyer cannot simply take over the seller's loan. In such cases, the mortgage must be paid off when the home is sold, and the buyer must secure their own financing.

1.3 Types of Loans That Can Be Assumed
Certain types of loans are more likely to be assumable, including:

- **FHA Loans**: Federal Housing Administration loans are often assumable, which can be advantageous when interest rates are high. The buyer may be able to assume the loan and benefit from a lower interest rate than what's available in the current market.
- **VA Loans**: Veterans Affairs loans are also typically assumable. VA loans offer favorable terms, and assuming the loan may allow the buyer to avoid the traditional application process.
- **USDA Loans**: Loans backed by the United States Department of Agriculture for rural properties can sometimes be assumed under certain conditions.
- **Conventional Loans**: While most conventional loans are not assumable, there are some exceptions. The buyer may need to negotiate with the lender to determine if assumption is possible.

Subsection 2: When Assumption Makes Sense

2.1 Buyer's Perspective
A mortgage assumption can make sense for a buyer in several scenarios:

How to Buy a House Without a Mortgage: Creative Financing Strategies

- **Lower Interest Rates**: If the seller has a low-interest-rate mortgage, assuming the loan can help the buyer lock in those favorable terms. This can be especially valuable in a rising-interest-rate environment where new mortgages may come with much higher rates.
- **Avoiding the Approval Process**: Mortgage assumptions can sometimes bypass the stringent approval process of traditional mortgages. If a buyer struggles with credit issues or a low down payment, assuming the seller's mortgage may be an easier path to homeownership.
- **Reducing Closing Costs**: With an assumption, the buyer may avoid many of the closing costs associated with a traditional mortgage. These costs can include lender fees, origination charges, and appraisal costs. Assuming a mortgage can save the buyer money.
- **Easier Process**: Mortgage assumption may be a quicker process than securing a new loan, especially if the buyer is able to meet the lender's qualifications for assuming the loan. In a hot real estate market, this can be an advantage for buyers looking to close quickly.

2.2 Seller's Perspective

From the seller's perspective, a mortgage assumption may be a good option under certain conditions:

- **Selling Faster**: Offering a home with an assumable mortgage can attract more buyers, especially in a market where mortgage rates are rising. Buyers who may have difficulty securing financing may find assuming an existing loan appealing.
- **Continuing the Loan**: In some cases, a seller may want to move quickly or reduce the debt burden, and offering an assumable mortgage can facilitate this. It may also allow them to walk away from the property without having to pay off the entire loan balance immediately.
- **Attracting More Buyers**: Sellers may find that offering an assumable mortgage increases the pool of potential buyers,

especially those who are already familiar with the terms of the existing mortgage and see it as a valuable option.

Subsection 3: Legal Considerations and Pitfalls

3.1 Lender Approval and Due-on-Sale Clause

One of the most important legal considerations in a mortgage assumption is the lender's approval. Many lenders include a **"due-on-sale"** clause in their mortgage contracts, which gives the lender the right to demand full repayment of the loan if the property is sold or transferred. This clause can prevent a buyer from assuming the mortgage unless the lender waives the clause or agrees to the assumption.

- **Due-on-Sale Clause**: If the lender's due-on-sale clause is triggered, the buyer may be required to pay off the entire balance of the mortgage or refinance the loan. This can be a significant obstacle to completing a mortgage assumption, especially if the buyer does not have the funds or credit to obtain a new mortgage.
- **Lender Approval**: Even if the loan is assumable, the lender must approve the assumption. This process often involves a review of the buyer's financial situation, including creditworthiness and income, to ensure they can afford the loan. If the buyer does not meet the lender's criteria, the assumption may not be approved.

3.2 Risks to Buyers

While assuming a mortgage can offer benefits, buyers should be aware of several potential risks:

- **Remaining Seller's Liability**: In some cases, the original borrower (the seller) may still be liable for the loan, even after the assumption. If the buyer defaults, the seller could be held responsible for the balance.

How to Buy a House Without a Mortgage: Creative Financing Strategies

- **Potential for Hidden Fees**: While assuming a mortgage can reduce closing costs, there may be hidden fees involved in the process, such as administrative fees or charges for modifying the mortgage agreement.
- **Property Condition and Inspection**: The condition of the property may be another consideration for the buyer. Unlike traditional financing where a buyer might get an inspection and appraisal, an assumption may not require the same level of scrutiny. Buyers should be cautious and ensure that they are not assuming a property with significant issues.

3.3 Risks to Sellers
Sellers also face certain risks when offering a mortgage assumption:

- **Responsibility for Default**: If the buyer defaults on the loan, the seller may still be responsible for the mortgage, especially if they are not fully released from liability by the lender.
- **Market Value**: If the buyer assumes the mortgage at a price below the current market value, the seller may not receive the full value they were hoping for. This could result in a situation where the seller is not fully compensated for the property.
- **Potential Complications with Lender**: If the lender does not approve the assumption or imposes strict conditions, the sale could fall through. Sellers should be prepared for potential delays or complications in the process.

Subsection 4: How to Find Homes with Assumable Mortgages

4.1 Working with Real Estate Agents
To find homes with assumable mortgages, buyers can start by working with a real estate agent who is familiar with creative financing strategies. A skilled agent can help identify homes with

assumable loans or properties that may be candidates for such arrangements.

4.2 Online Listings and Marketplaces
Some online real estate platforms may allow buyers to filter for homes with assumable mortgages, or sellers may advertise these types of properties specifically. Buyers should look for listings that mention "assumable mortgage" or "owner financing" as part of the property description.

4.3 Directly Contacting Sellers
Buyers can also explore assumable mortgage opportunities by directly contacting homeowners in areas they are interested in. Homeowners who are facing foreclosure or looking to sell quickly may be open to discussing the possibility of a mortgage assumption.

4.4 Exploring Government-Backed Loans
Government-backed loans, such as FHA, VA, and USDA loans, are more likely to be assumable. Buyers should specifically search for homes with these types of loans, as the terms are more favorable for assumption.

Conclusion

Mortgage assumption is a powerful and often overlooked strategy for buying a home without a traditional mortgage. It offers benefits for both buyers and sellers, allowing for easier financing and the potential to lock in favorable loan terms. However, it's important to carefully consider the legal, financial, and logistical aspects of mortgage assumptions. This chapter has provided a comprehensive overview of how mortgage assumption works, when it makes sense, the risks involved, and how to find homes with assumable mortgages. By fully understanding this strategy, buyers and sellers can make informed decisions and explore a debt-free path to homeownership.

41 How to Buy a House Without a Mortgage: Creative Financing Strategies

Chapter 6: Lease Options and Lease Purchase Agreements

In creative financing, lease options and lease purchase agreements provide unique ways to buy a house without a mortgage. These two methods allow buyers to control a property for a certain period before deciding to purchase, offering flexible solutions for those who are not yet ready to commit to traditional home financing. This chapter explains the intricacies of lease options and lease purchase agreements, how they work, the differences between them, and the pros and cons for buyers.

Subsection 1: What is a Lease Option?

1.1 Definition of a Lease Option
A lease option is a real estate agreement in which the buyer rents a property with the option to purchase it at a later date, usually within a specified time frame (e.g., 1-3 years). This type of agreement provides the buyer with the flexibility to choose whether or not they want to buy the property, typically at a predetermined price. The buyer is not obligated to purchase the property but has the right to do so at their discretion.

1.2 Structure of a Lease Option
In a lease option agreement, there are two main components:

- **Lease Agreement**: The buyer rents the property from the seller, typically for a set period. The rent is paid as usual, but part of the payment may be credited toward the eventual purchase price.
- **Option to Purchase**: The buyer has the option (but not the obligation) to buy the property during or at the end of the lease term. This is usually done at a pre-agreed price that is established at the start of the lease agreement.

1.3 How Lease Options Work in Practice

The lease option structure benefits both buyers and sellers:

- **For Buyers**: The lease option provides an opportunity to live in the home while preserving the right to purchase it later. This can be advantageous for individuals who are not financially prepared to buy immediately but expect to be ready in the future.
- **For Sellers**: The seller may attract tenants who are interested in eventually purchasing the home, offering the seller a steady stream of rental income while retaining the option to sell.

1.4 Common Lease Option Terms

- **Option Fee**: The buyer typically pays a non-refundable option fee upfront for the right to purchase the property. This fee can range from 1-5% of the property's value and is typically applied to the purchase price if the buyer decides to exercise the option.
- **Lease Terms**: Rent is usually slightly higher than market value, with a portion of it credited toward the purchase price.
- **Purchase Price**: The purchase price is agreed upon at the beginning of the agreement, providing clarity and stability for both parties.

Subsection 2: How to Structure a Lease Purchase Agreement

2.1 What is a Lease Purchase Agreement?

A lease purchase agreement is similar to a lease option, but with one key difference: in a lease purchase agreement, the buyer is obligated to purchase the property at the end of the lease term, rather than having the option to do so. This structure is often used when the buyer is certain they will be able to buy the property but needs time to prepare for the purchase, such as saving for a down payment or improving their credit score.

2.2 Components of a Lease Purchase Agreement

- **Lease Terms**: As with a lease option, the buyer rents the property for a set period, with the rent payments often higher than market value. A portion of these payments may be credited toward the purchase price.
- **Purchase Obligation**: Unlike a lease option, the lease purchase agreement obligates the buyer to purchase the property at the end of the lease term. The purchase price is typically agreed upon at the start of the agreement and may include provisions for adjustment depending on market conditions.
- **Down Payment**: In many cases, the lease purchase agreement requires the buyer to provide a larger upfront down payment or an initial deposit that will be credited toward the final purchase price.

2.3 When Lease Purchase Agreements Work Best

Lease purchase agreements are typically used when:

- The buyer is ready and committed to purchasing the property but needs time to prepare financially.
- The seller is confident that the buyer will follow through with the purchase and is looking for more certainty than a lease option arrangement provides.
- Both parties are clear about the terms and conditions, which should be well defined to avoid conflicts later.

2.4 Negotiating the Terms of a Lease Purchase Agreement

When structuring a lease purchase agreement, it's essential to outline clear terms for both the buyer and the seller. Key aspects to negotiate include:

- **Rent**: The rental price should reflect market value or higher, with a portion of the rent credited toward the eventual purchase.

- **Purchase Price**: The purchase price should be agreed upon at the outset, and it's often beneficial to negotiate a fixed price rather than one that can fluctuate based on market conditions.
- **Deposit**: A larger upfront deposit or down payment may be required, which could be credited toward the purchase price when the agreement concludes.
- **Option to Extend**: While the lease purchase agreement typically sets a fixed end date for purchasing the property, it may be worth negotiating an option for extending the lease if the buyer needs additional time to finalize their financing.

Subsection 3: Key Differences Between Rent-to-Own and Lease Options

3.1 Understanding Rent-to-Own

A rent-to-own agreement is a hybrid contract that combines elements of a rental agreement with an option to purchase the property at the end of the rental period. Unlike a lease option, rent-to-own agreements are typically structured in such a way that the buyer is more committed to eventually purchasing the property.

3.2 Key Differences Between Rent-to-Own and Lease Option Agreements

The primary differences between rent-to-own and lease option agreements include:

- **Obligation to Buy**: In a lease option agreement, the buyer has the right but not the obligation to purchase the home. In a rent-to-own agreement, the buyer is usually obligated to buy the property at the end of the term.
- **Rent vs. Rent Credit**: Rent-to-own agreements often require the buyer to pay a higher rent, but a larger portion of the payment is credited toward the purchase price. In a lease option, only a small portion of the rent might be credited.

How to Buy a House Without a Mortgage: Creative Financing Strategies

- **Commitment Level**: Rent-to-own agreements are more binding, as the buyer is usually expected to follow through with the purchase. Lease options are more flexible and allow the buyer to walk away without penalty.

3.3 Which Option Is Better?

The decision between rent-to-own and lease option agreements depends on the buyer's commitment level and financial readiness:

- **Lease Option**: Ideal for buyers who are uncertain about their ability to purchase or who want the flexibility to walk away at the end of the lease term.
- **Rent-to-Own**: Suitable for buyers who are committed to purchasing but need time to prepare financially or stabilize their credit.

Subsection 4: Pros and Cons for Buyers

4.1 Pros of Lease Options for Buyers

- **Flexibility**: Buyers have the option, but not the obligation, to purchase the property, giving them time to decide whether it is the right investment.
- **Lock in Purchase Price**: Lease options allow the buyer to lock in the purchase price at the beginning of the lease term, which can be beneficial in a rising market.
- **Credit Building**: The lease portion of the agreement can be structured to help buyers build credit or save for a down payment while living in the property.
- **Control of the Property**: Lease options allow the buyer to live in the home and control the property while preparing for a future purchase.

4.2 Cons of Lease Options for Buyers

- **Non-Refundable Option Fee**: The option fee paid upfront is usually non-refundable, meaning that if the buyer decides not to purchase, they lose this money.
- **Higher Rent**: Rent may be higher than market value, which could make it more difficult for buyers to afford.
- **Limited Control Over Purchase**: While the buyer can choose not to purchase, they may lose the opportunity if the property is sold to someone else during the lease period.

4.3 Pros of Lease Purchase Agreements for Buyers

- **Commitment to Buy**: Buyers who are sure about purchasing the property have the security of a binding contract that obligates the purchase, which provides clarity.
- **Rent Credit Toward Purchase**: A portion of the rent goes toward the purchase price, which can help buyers build equity while renting.
- **Time to Prepare**: Lease purchase agreements give buyers time to improve their financial situation before purchasing.

4.4 Cons of Lease Purchase Agreements for Buyers

- **Obligation to Buy**: Unlike a lease option, a lease purchase agreement requires the buyer to purchase the home at the end of the lease term, which can be problematic if their financial situation changes or if they decide they no longer want the property.
- **Higher Upfront Costs**: Lease purchase agreements may require larger upfront deposits, which could be a barrier for some buyers.
- **Risk of Losing Investment**: If the buyer does not exercise the purchase option, they may lose all the money invested in rent credits and upfront deposits.

Conclusion

47 How to Buy a House Without a Mortgage: Creative Financing Strategies

Lease options and lease purchase agreements offer buyers alternative pathways to homeownership without relying on traditional mortgages. These creative financing strategies provide flexibility and opportunities to prepare financially while living in the home. While there are advantages, such as building credit, locking in a purchase price, and saving for a down payment, buyers must carefully consider the potential downsides, such as non-refundable fees, higher rent, and the risk of losing their investment. Understanding the differences between these options and the pros and cons is essential for making an informed decision that aligns with a buyer's financial situation and long-term goals.

Chapter 7: Using Home Equity for Financing

Using home equity as a means of financing a new home purchase is one of the most strategic ways to avoid taking on traditional mortgage debt. Home equity refers to the portion of a property's value that the homeowner actually owns, which can be leveraged for various financial purposes. In this chapter, we will explore how home equity can be utilized as a powerful tool in creative financing, allowing buyers to purchase a new home or refinance their current home without the need for a conventional mortgage. We will also discuss equity sharing agreements, the risks, and rewards of equity-based financing, and how home equity can open alternative paths to homeownership.

Subsection 1: Understanding Home Equity

1.1 Definition of Home Equity
Home equity is the difference between the current market value of your home and the outstanding balance of any mortgages or loans on the property. In simple terms, home equity represents the amount of the property you actually "own" and is considered a valuable financial asset. For example, if your home is worth $300,000 and you owe $200,000 on your mortgage, your home equity is $100,000.

1.2 How Home Equity Builds Over Time
Home equity builds in two ways:

- **Appreciation**: If your home's value increases over time due to market conditions or improvements, your equity grows.
- **Mortgage Payments**: As you pay off your mortgage, the principal balance reduces, which also increases your equity.

For homeowners who have been in their property for several years, home equity can accumulate significantly, providing opportunities to

How to Buy a House Without a Mortgage: Creative Financing Strategies

access funds for future investments, including purchasing a new home.

1.3 How to Calculate Home Equity
To calculate your home equity, simply subtract the remaining mortgage balance from your home's current market value:

- Home Equity = Market Value of Home - Remaining Mortgage Balance

Understanding this calculation is essential, as it helps homeowners determine how much equity they can potentially use in creative financing strategies like using home equity for the purchase of a new home.

1.4 Benefits of Building Home Equity

- **Increased Borrowing Power**: A larger equity stake in your home can increase your borrowing potential, making it easier to secure financing for future investments.
- **Financial Security**: Equity represents ownership in your property, which can be accessed during financial hardship or when looking for alternative home financing options.
- **Potential for Profit**: As property values rise, so too does your equity, which can translate to substantial profit when selling.

Subsection 2: How to Use Home Equity for a New Home Purchase

2.1 Home Equity Line of Credit (HELOC)
A Home Equity Line of Credit (HELOC) is a revolving line of credit that allows you to borrow against your home equity. It functions similarly to a credit card, offering flexibility to borrow and repay funds as needed. If you're looking to purchase a new home, a

HELOC could provide the necessary capital for a down payment or even cover the entire cost of a new property, depending on the amount of equity available.

2.2 Home Equity Loan

A Home Equity Loan (HEL) is another way to leverage your home equity for a new home purchase. Unlike a HELOC, a home equity loan provides a lump sum amount, which is typically used for specific purposes, such as buying a second home or purchasing a primary residence. With a home equity loan, the borrower typically receives a fixed interest rate, making it easier to predict monthly payments.

Home equity loans are often used when buyers need a larger sum of money upfront for a new home purchase but want to avoid the complexities of a traditional mortgage.

2.3 Pros and Cons of Using Home Equity for a New Home Purchase

- **Pros**:
    - **Lower Interest Rates**: Interest rates on HELOCs and home equity loans are typically lower than those on traditional mortgages, as the home serves as collateral.
    - **No Traditional Mortgage Required**: Using home equity eliminates the need for a conventional mortgage, which can be beneficial for those with poor credit or who are looking for faster approval.
    - **Flexibility**: With a HELOC, buyers can borrow money as needed and only pay interest on what they use.
- **Cons**:
    - **Risk of Foreclosure**: Because the home is used as collateral, failure to repay the loan could result in foreclosure.

51 How to Buy a House Without a Mortgage: Creative Financing Strategies

- o **Variable Interest Rates**: HELOCs often have variable interest rates, which can increase over time, making payments unpredictable.
- o **Limited to Available Equity**: The amount of equity you can use is directly tied to the value of your property, which could limit your options if the equity is not sufficient.

2.4 How to Use Home Equity to Buy a New Home Without a Traditional Mortgage

For many buyers, the idea of using home equity to purchase a new home may seem risky, but it can be an ideal solution for those with significant equity in their current property. Buyers can:

- Use their equity to secure a HELOC or home equity loan for a down payment or full purchase.
- Buy a new home outright by using home equity to pay for the full price, which allows them to avoid mortgages entirely.
- Use home equity in conjunction with other creative financing strategies, such as seller financing or rent-to-own agreements, to minimize debt and interest obligations.

Subsection 3: Equity Sharing Agreements

3.1 What is an Equity Sharing Agreement?

An equity sharing agreement is a partnership between two parties, typically a buyer and an investor, where both share the ownership of a property. This agreement allows the buyer to purchase a home without a traditional mortgage by leveraging their equity in another property or with the help of an investor.

The buyer usually contributes part of the equity for the down payment, while the investor covers the remaining costs, such as the mortgage or additional property expenses. Over time, both parties benefit as the home's value appreciates, and the buyer gradually increases their stake in the property.

3.2 Structure of an Equity Sharing Agreement
In an equity share, the agreement often includes:

- **Initial Contributions**: The buyer contributes a portion of the down payment, while the investor provides the remainder or funds the mortgage.
- **Ownership Split**: The buyer typically owns a percentage of the property, based on their initial contribution, while the investor holds the remainder.
- **Profit Sharing**: When the property is sold, the profits from the sale are divided according to the ownership split, with the buyer and investor both receiving their respective shares.

3.3 When to Use an Equity Share Agreement
Equity share agreements are particularly useful for buyers who:

- Have limited savings for a down payment but have good credit and the ability to pay ongoing costs.
- Want to purchase a property without taking on a mortgage themselves.
- Are looking for a lower-risk method of homeownership with an investor partner.

Subsection 4: Risks and Rewards of Equity-Based Financing

4.1 Risks of Equity-Based Financing

- **Risk of Foreclosure**: As with any secured loan, failing to meet payment obligations could result in the loss of the property.

How to Buy a House Without a Mortgage: Creative Financing Strategies

- **Debt Accumulation**: Although home equity loans or lines of credit offer lower interest rates, they still result in new debt, which must be managed responsibly to avoid financial strain.
- **Over-leveraging**: Borrowing too much against your home's equity may lead to a situation where the property is "over-leveraged," making it difficult to sell or refinance in the future.
- **Dividing Profits**: In an equity-sharing agreement, any profits from selling the property are shared, which means that the buyer may not see the full financial benefit from the sale of the property.

4.2 Rewards of Equity-Based Financing

- **Access to Capital**: Home equity provides a unique opportunity to access capital that can be used for purchasing a new home without taking on high-interest debt.
- **Reduced Financial Barriers**: For buyers who have built up equity in their current home, this form of financing allows them to sidestep the restrictions of a traditional mortgage.
- **Flexibility and Lower Costs**: With lower interest rates and more flexible repayment options than traditional mortgages, home equity loans and lines of credit can be an affordable and efficient way to finance a new home.

Conclusion

Using home equity for financing provides a valuable alternative to traditional mortgage pathways, offering flexibility and lower costs for buyers with sufficient equity in their property. Whether through a Home Equity Line of Credit (HELOC), home equity loan, or equity-sharing agreements, homeowners can leverage their existing property to buy a new home, expand their investment portfolio, or reduce debt. While there are risks involved, particularly with over-leveraging and potential foreclosure, the rewards can be substantial, providing

54   How to Buy a House Without a Mortgage: Creative Financing Strategies

an accessible route to homeownership for many. Understanding how to use home equity effectively can be a key tool in navigating creative financing strategies and achieving homeownership without the burden of a traditional mortgage.

How to Buy a House Without a Mortgage: Creative Financing Strategies

Chapter 8: Crowdfunding Your Home Purchase

Crowdfunding is a modern and innovative approach to financing that enables individuals to pool money from a large number of people, typically via the internet, to fund a project or investment. In the case of homeownership, crowdfunding offers an alternative to traditional methods of securing a mortgage. This chapter delves into how crowdfunding for real estate works, how to set up a real estate crowdfunding campaign, the legal considerations involved, and shares successful case studies of individuals who have used crowdfunding to purchase their homes.

Subsection 1: How Crowdfunding for Real Estate Works

1.1 Definition of Crowdfunding for Real Estate
Crowdfunding for real estate is the process of raising small amounts of capital from a large group of investors, typically via an online platform, to fund the purchase or development of a property. For homebuyers, this could mean gathering the necessary funds for a down payment, full purchase, or renovation of a home.

Crowdfunding for real estate often involves two main models:

- **Equity Crowdfunding**: Investors contribute money in exchange for an ownership stake in the property, meaning they share in the profits or losses when the property is sold or rented out.
- **Debt Crowdfunding**: Investors contribute money as lenders rather than owners, and in return, they receive regular interest payments and principal repayments.

1.2 The Rise of Crowdfunding Platforms
Crowdfunding for real estate has grown substantially due to the development of online platforms such as Fundrise, RealtyShares, and Crowdstreet, which connect buyers with potential investors. These

platforms enable buyers to present their real estate investment projects to a wide audience, and individuals can choose to invest as little or as much as they wish.

1.3 The Mechanics of Crowdfunding

Typically, a homeowner or investor looking to purchase a property sets up a crowdfunding campaign on an online platform. They detail the goals of the campaign, provide information about the property, and outline how the funds will be used. Potential investors can then browse various campaigns and choose which ones they wish to invest in.

Once enough money is raised to meet the target goal, the campaign is closed, and the funds are used for the home purchase. Depending on the model chosen, the investors may become partial owners or receive interest payments on the money they invested.

1.4 Benefits of Crowdfunding for Home Purchases

- **Access to Capital**: Crowdfunding allows buyers to access funding from a large group of people, which can be particularly helpful for individuals who may not have the savings or financial history required for traditional home loans.
- **Low Barriers to Entry**: The ease of setting up a campaign and the ability to contribute small amounts of money make it accessible to a wider range of people, both buyers and investors.
- **Flexible Terms**: Crowdfunding campaigns can be tailored to meet the needs of both buyers and investors, with different payout structures and investment terms.

Subsection 2: Setting Up a Real Estate Crowdfunding Campaign

57 How to Buy a House Without a Mortgage: Creative Financing Strategies

2.1 Identifying Your Goals and Property Needs

Before setting up a crowdfunding campaign for your home purchase, it is essential to clearly define your goals. Are you looking to raise funds for a down payment? Do you need financing for a full purchase or renovation of a property? Clearly defining the purpose of your campaign will help you attract the right investors and set appropriate fundraising targets.

It is also important to ensure that the property you are purchasing aligns with the crowdfunding model. For instance, if you are seeking funds for a rental property or fixer-upper, you may want to include a clear business plan outlining how you intend to generate returns for your investors.

2.2 Choosing a Crowdfunding Platform

There are several crowdfunding platforms available that specialize in real estate investments. Choosing the right platform for your needs is critical. Some platforms focus on equity crowdfunding, while others may specialize in debt crowdfunding or even niche areas like green or sustainable real estate investments.

Popular real estate crowdfunding platforms include:

- **Fundrise**: Specializes in real estate investment trusts (REITs), allowing investors to contribute to a diversified pool of properties.
- **RealtyShares**: Focuses on both residential and commercial properties, offering debt and equity investments.
- **Groundfloor**: A platform that allows smaller investments in real estate development projects and home renovations.

2.3 Creating a Campaign

Once you have chosen a platform, the next step is to create your crowdfunding campaign. The campaign will require detailed information about:

- **The Property**: Including its location, size, current value, and potential for appreciation.
- **Your Story**: Share your journey and why you're using crowdfunding to purchase your home. Investors are more likely to contribute if they feel personally connected to the campaign.
- **The Financials**: Detail how much money you need to raise and how the funds will be used. Include any expected timelines for repayment or returns.

You will also need to offer incentives to potential investors, whether in the form of equity ownership or promised returns on their contributions.

2.4 Marketing and Promotion of the Campaign

Successfully promoting your campaign is crucial to attracting investors. Marketing strategies can include:

- **Social Media Outreach**: Use platforms like Facebook, Instagram, and LinkedIn to reach out to potential investors.
- **Email Newsletters**: Engage with your network and encourage them to share the campaign with their circles.
- **Crowdfunding Communities**: Many crowdfunding platforms have built-in communities of investors who actively seek out investment opportunities. Engaging with these communities can help boost your campaign's visibility.

2.5 Managing and Closing the Campaign

Once the funding goal has been met, the campaign is considered successful. From there, you will need to manage the funds, ensuring they are used for their intended purpose. Keeping investors updated on the progress of your property purchase is important, especially if they are equity investors who will be expecting returns.

If you don't meet the funding goal, the campaign may be considered unsuccessful, and funds will typically be refunded to the investors.

How to Buy a House Without a Mortgage: Creative Financing Strategies

Subsection 3: Legal Aspects of Crowdfunding

3.1 Regulatory Framework for Crowdfunding
Crowdfunding, particularly for real estate, is governed by a variety of laws and regulations. In the United States, for example, crowdfunding for real estate investments is regulated by the **Securities and Exchange Commission (SEC)**, which ensures that campaigns follow rules intended to protect investors.

- **Regulation Crowdfunding**: Under the JOBS Act (Jumpstart Our Business Startups Act), small businesses and individuals can raise capital through crowdfunding, provided they adhere to certain rules, such as not exceeding a set amount of funds and disclosing financial information to investors.
- **Accredited vs. Non-Accredited Investors**: Many crowdfunding platforms limit investments to accredited investors (those with higher income or net worth), although some platforms allow non-accredited investors to participate in certain campaigns.

3.2 Structuring Legal Agreements
When setting up a crowdfunding campaign, legal agreements will be necessary, especially if investors are being offered an ownership stake in the property or a share of the rental income. These agreements typically include:

- **Investment Contracts**: Detailing the terms of the investment, including the amount of capital being raised, the percentage of ownership or return on investment, and any rights or responsibilities of the investors.
- **Equity Share Agreements**: If you are offering equity, a legal agreement will outline the ownership percentages, the distribution of profits, and the process for selling the property.

3.3 Tax Considerations

Real estate crowdfunding can have tax implications for both the buyers and the investors. For buyers, it is important to consult with a tax professional to understand how using crowdfunding to purchase a home will affect their tax liabilities. Investors, too, should be informed about how their returns will be taxed, depending on whether they are receiving equity shares or interest payments.

Subsection 4: Successful Case Studies of Crowdfunding for Homeownership

4.1 Case Study 1: The Crowdfunded First-Time Homebuyer

In this case, a first-time homebuyer was able to raise $150,000 through crowdfunding to purchase their home in a competitive real estate market. By offering equity in the property, the buyer attracted a group of investors who were interested in the property's long-term value. This campaign was successful due to its compelling story, the property's strong investment potential, and effective marketing through social media.

4.2 Case Study 2: Using Crowdfunding for Home Renovation

Another case involved an investor who used crowdfunding to finance the purchase and renovation of a home. By offering debt financing to investors, they were able to raise the necessary capital to buy the property and make necessary repairs. Investors were promised a fixed interest return over a 12-month period, and the project was completed successfully, with the home being sold for a significant profit.

4.3 Lessons Learned from Successful Crowdfunding Campaigns

- **Clear Goals**: Campaigns that clearly define the purpose of the funding, whether for a down payment, full purchase, or renovation, are more likely to succeed.

- **Compelling Story**: Buyers who are able to convey a personal connection to the home or investment project often attract more support.
- **Transparency**: Successful campaigns provide detailed financial information and regular updates to investors, creating trust and maintaining momentum.

Conclusion

Crowdfunding for real estate represents a modern and creative financing solution for those looking to buy a home without a traditional mortgage. By leveraging the power of a large pool of small investors, buyers can gain access to capital that would otherwise be out of reach. Through effective campaign strategies, understanding the legal landscape, and learning from successful case studies, crowdfunding can open new doors for homeownership and provide an alternative path for those seeking financial independence and debt-free living.

How to Buy a House Without a Mortgage: Creative Financing Strategies

Chapter 9: Bartering and Alternative Exchanges

Bartering, the practice of exchanging goods or services without using money, has existed for centuries. In the modern world, while money-based transactions are dominant, bartering remains a viable and creative option for buying a home without relying on traditional mortgage financing. This chapter delves into the concept of bartering in real estate, how to structure a property barter agreement, finding opportunities to barter for property, and the legal and tax implications of bartering real estate.

Subsection 1: The Concept of Bartering in Real Estate

1.1 What is Bartering?

Bartering is the exchange of goods or services directly for other goods or services, without the use of money or credit. Traditionally, bartering involved a person trading an item or service of value for another item or service they needed. In the context of real estate, bartering refers to the exchange of property or services for another property or service, bypassing the need for traditional financial transactions.

1.2 The Role of Bartering in Real Estate Transactions

Bartering in real estate is an alternative financing strategy where two parties agree to exchange properties or services instead of using cash. This arrangement may be beneficial when one or both parties cannot access or do not want to use traditional financing, like mortgages. Bartering can help overcome financial limitations, ease the property acquisition process, and create win-win situations for both parties.

For example, a homeowner might offer a piece of land or a home they own in exchange for a property with different features or in a different location. Alternatively, services, such as construction work or home repairs, might be used as part of the barter arrangement.

How to Buy a House Without a Mortgage: Creative Financing Strategies

1.3 Types of Barter in Real Estate
There are various forms of bartering in real estate, including:

- **Property-for-Property Exchange**: This is the most straightforward form of real estate bartering. One person offers their property in exchange for another property.
- **Services-for-Property Exchange**: Sometimes, services like renovation, landscaping, or even professional services (e.g., legal, consulting) can be exchanged for property.
- **Mixed-Value Bartering**: A combination of property and services is exchanged, with one party adding a cash payment or additional services to balance the value of the transaction.

1.4 Why Barter for Real Estate?
Bartering can be particularly useful in situations where traditional financing options are limited. Some reasons buyers and sellers may choose to barter for property include:

- **Lack of Access to Capital**: Buyers may not have enough cash for a down payment or a mortgage but still have valuable assets they can trade.
- **Property Equity**: Homeowners may wish to downsize or exchange their current home for one that better suits their needs or lifestyle, and bartering allows for this exchange without involving a third-party lender.
- **Avoiding Debt**: For individuals looking to purchase a home without taking on debt, bartering provides an attractive option to acquire property without financial obligations.
- **Market Conditions**: In some cases, a downturn in the market may make it difficult to sell a property for cash. Bartering can provide a viable exit strategy.

Subsection 2: How to Structure a Property Barter Agreement

2.1 Creating a Barter Agreement

A barter agreement is a contract that formalizes the terms of the exchange between two parties. This agreement serves as a legal document that outlines the specifics of the transaction, ensuring that both parties understand their obligations and responsibilities. When structuring a property barter agreement, several elements should be included:

- **Description of the Properties**: Clearly identify the properties being exchanged, including addresses, legal descriptions, and any relevant details about the properties' conditions.
- **Valuation**: Agree on how the value of each property will be assessed. Typically, an appraisal or property inspection is required to establish a fair market value for each property.
- **Additional Considerations**: If the properties are of unequal value, discuss how to balance the difference. This may involve a cash payment (known as "cash to balance") or the exchange of services.
- **Timeline for Completion**: Establish a timeline for completing the transaction, including deadlines for inspections, appraisals, and finalizing the paperwork.
- **Contingencies**: Include any contingencies that may affect the transaction, such as financing approval for the buyer's property or repairs to be made to one of the properties before the exchange can occur.
- **Title and Ownership Transfer**: Detail the process by which the titles of the properties will be transferred, and include any legal formalities that must be met to ensure the transaction is complete.

2.2 Legal Requirements for Barter Transactions

While barter transactions may seem informal, they still need to adhere to legal requirements to ensure their validity. Both parties should consult with legal professionals to ensure that the agreement complies with local laws and regulations. The following legal requirements must be considered:

- **Title and Ownership Transfer**: As with traditional real estate transactions, a title transfer must occur to ensure that ownership rights are legally transferred from one party to the other.
- **Disclosure of Property Conditions**: Both parties must disclose any known defects or issues with the properties involved in the exchange. Failure to disclose can result in legal disputes after the transaction is completed.
- **Notarization**: Some jurisdictions may require that the barter agreement be notarized to validate the contract. Check local regulations to ensure that proper procedures are followed.

2.3 Closing the Deal
Once all the terms have been agreed upon and both parties are satisfied, the final step is closing the deal. A professional real estate agent, lawyer, or notary can help facilitate this process. The properties are transferred, and all necessary paperwork is completed, just as in a traditional sale.

Subsection 3: Finding Opportunities to Barter for Property

3.1 Where to Find Property Barter Opportunities
Bartering for real estate requires creativity and proactive searching. Not all sellers or buyers are open to bartering, so identifying the right opportunities is crucial. Some of the best places to find barter opportunities include:

- **Real Estate Listings**: Some sellers may explicitly state that they are open to bartering in their property listings. Look for ads that mention flexible payment options or "cash or trade" offers.
- **Real Estate Networks**: Networking with other buyers, sellers, and real estate professionals is one of the most effective ways to find barter opportunities. Local real estate investment groups or online forums can be great resources.

- **Classified Ads and Social Media**: Platforms such as Craigslist, Facebook Marketplace, and local community boards can feature barter offers or exchanges.
- **Word of Mouth**: Sometimes, the best opportunities come from personal connections. Let friends, family, and colleagues know you are interested in property bartering, and they may be able to point you to potential sellers or buyers.

3.2 Negotiating a Barter Agreement

Negotiating a barter agreement can be more complex than a traditional cash transaction. Buyers and sellers need to be flexible, open to alternative arrangements, and willing to compromise. Here are a few tips for successful negotiations:

- **Determine Your Needs**: Understand what you need from the exchange, whether it's acquiring a specific property, avoiding debt, or exchanging services.
- **Establish Value**: Make sure both parties agree on the value of the properties involved. Fairness in valuation is key to a successful barter.
- **Be Open to Compromise**: Since the value of properties can vary, be prepared to offer or accept a combination of property and services to balance the deal.

Subsection 4: The Legal and Tax Implications of Bartering Real Estate

4.1 Legal Considerations in Bartering Real Estate

Bartering for property is legal in most places, but it is essential to follow the legal processes that govern property transactions. Some specific legal considerations include:

- **Contract Law**: Bartering agreements should comply with the principles of contract law. This includes mutual consent, capacity, consideration, and legality of the terms.

How to Buy a House Without a Mortgage: Creative Financing Strategies

- **State and Local Real Estate Laws**: Ensure that your barter agreement complies with the real estate laws of your state or locality, especially with respect to property transfer processes, disclosure requirements, and tax regulations.
- **Title Transfer and Registration**: Property title transfers must be properly executed and recorded with local authorities to ensure legal ownership is established.

4.2 Tax Implications of Bartering

Bartering real estate transactions can have significant tax implications. Both parties may be subject to capital gains tax or other tax liabilities, depending on the nature of the transaction and the jurisdictions involved:

- **Taxable Event**: Bartering property is considered a taxable event by the IRS. Both buyers and sellers must report the transaction on their tax returns.
- **Fair Market Value**: The fair market value of the property or services exchanged must be reported for tax purposes. Both parties may need to provide documentation to substantiate the value.
- **Capital Gains Tax**: If either party sells or exchanges property that has appreciated in value, they may be subject to capital gains tax on the profit from the sale or exchange.

4.3 Consulting a Tax Professional

Because bartering involves unique tax challenges, it is advisable to consult with a tax professional or accountant who can help navigate the tax implications of a property barter exchange.

Conclusion

Bartering for property is a creative, debt-free alternative to traditional home financing. While it may not be as common as using a mortgage, bartering offers a unique opportunity to acquire property or exchange services without relying on cash or loans. By understanding how to structure barter agreements, finding the right opportunities, and considering the legal and tax implications, buyers and sellers can make successful property exchanges that benefit both parties.

69 How to Buy a House Without a Mortgage: Creative Financing Strategies

Chapter 10: Peer-to-Peer Lending and Private Loans

Peer-to-peer (P2P) lending and private loans have emerged as innovative, flexible alternatives to traditional mortgage financing, enabling homebuyers to access funding directly from individuals or private institutions, bypassing conventional financial intermediaries like banks. These options provide creative ways to buy a house without relying on the standard mortgage process. This chapter explores how peer-to-peer lending and private loans work, how to find the right lenders, loan structures and terms, and how to assess risks and protect investments in these financing methods.

Subsection 1: How Peer-to-Peer Lending Works for Homebuyers

1.1 What is Peer-to-Peer Lending?

Peer-to-peer lending is a method of borrowing and lending money directly between individuals, bypassing traditional financial institutions such as banks and credit unions. Through online platforms, borrowers (homebuyers) can connect with individual lenders (investors) who are willing to provide funds in exchange for an interest return.

P2P lending platforms typically act as intermediaries, facilitating the connection, loan agreements, and transactions between borrowers and lenders. Examples of P2P lending platforms include LendingClub, Prosper, and Funding Circle. These platforms assess the borrower's creditworthiness and offer different loan options, which often come with more flexible terms and interest rates compared to traditional financial institutions.

1.2 How P2P Lending Works for Homebuyers

When it comes to buying a house without a traditional mortgage, P2P lending can provide homebuyers with access to alternative funding. Here's how it typically works:

1. **Loan Application**: A homebuyer applies for a loan through a P2P lending platform, providing details such as the loan amount needed, purpose (in this case, purchasing a property), and financial history.
2. **Credit Assessment**: The platform assesses the borrower's creditworthiness based on financial data such as income, credit score, and debt-to-income ratio.
3. **Matching with Lenders**: Once approved, the platform matches the borrower with potential lenders who are willing to provide the necessary funds. Homebuyers may receive multiple loan offers.
4. **Loan Terms Agreement**: The borrower and lenders agree on the terms of the loan, such as the interest rate, repayment schedule, and loan amount. The platform typically takes a small fee for its services.
5. **Receiving Funds**: Once the loan is approved and the terms are set, the borrower receives the funds, and the loan is used to purchase the property. The borrower repays the loan with interest according to the agreed-upon schedule.

P2P lending is appealing to homebuyers who may not qualify for traditional mortgages due to issues like credit history or the desire for more flexible terms.

1.3 Benefits of Peer-to-Peer Lending for Homebuyers

- **Flexibility**: P2P loans typically offer more flexible terms than traditional banks, such as adjustable repayment periods, lower fees, and the ability to negotiate interest rates.
- **Accessibility**: It can be easier to qualify for P2P loans, especially for borrowers with less-than-perfect credit, as the platforms take a more personalized approach to assessing risk.
- **Lower Interest Rates**: In some cases, borrowers can secure lower interest rates than those offered by banks or credit unions.

How to Buy a House Without a Mortgage: Creative Financing Strategies

Subsection 2: Finding the Right Private Lenders

2.1 What is a Private Lender?

A private lender is an individual or institution (such as a private equity firm, real estate investor, or family member) that lends money directly to homebuyers or real estate investors. Unlike traditional financial institutions, private lenders are more flexible in their lending criteria and terms. They may focus more on the value of the property being purchased rather than solely on the borrower's credit history.

Private lenders can be a good alternative for homebuyers who are looking for creative financing options. They can provide loans for home purchases, renovations, or even unconventional property types that banks may not be willing to finance.

2.2 How to Find the Right Private Lenders

Finding the right private lender involves conducting research, networking, and utilizing platforms that connect borrowers with private lenders. Here are some common ways to find private lenders:

- **Real Estate Investment Groups**: Many private lenders are part of real estate investment groups or networks where they offer funding to homebuyers and investors. These groups may meet in person or online, providing opportunities to build relationships with lenders.
- **Online Lending Platforms**: In addition to peer-to-peer platforms, some websites and apps connect homebuyers with private lenders, such as Groundfloor or PeerStreet. These platforms make it easier for buyers to find a variety of lending options.
- **Real Estate Agents and Brokers**: Some real estate professionals have connections with private lenders or may recommend lenders who specialize in non-traditional financing.

- **Friends and Family**: In some cases, homebuyers may choose to seek private funding from friends or family members who are willing to lend money for a home purchase.
- **Hard Money Lenders**: Hard money lenders are a type of private lender who offers short-term loans for real estate transactions, often secured by the property itself. These lenders typically focus on the property's value rather than the borrower's creditworthiness.

2.3 Key Considerations When Choosing a Private Lender

- **Reputation and Experience**: It's essential to choose a private lender with a solid reputation and experience in real estate lending. A trustworthy lender will offer fair terms and will work with you to structure a deal that fits your needs.
- **Loan Terms**: Review the terms the lender offers, including interest rates, repayment schedules, and fees. Private lenders may offer more flexible terms, but it's essential to ensure that the terms are reasonable and affordable.
- **Security and Collateral**: Many private lenders may require the property to serve as collateral for the loan. It's important to understand the implications of this in case of default.

Subsection 3: Loan Structures and Terms for Property Financing

3.1 Types of Loan Structures
Private loans for real estate can be structured in various ways, depending on the agreement between the borrower and the lender. Common loan structures include:

- **Interest-Only Loans**: This structure allows the borrower to pay only the interest on the loan for a specified period (often 5–10 years). After this period, the borrower will pay off the principal.

- **Fixed-Rate Loans**: Like a traditional mortgage, the loan has a fixed interest rate and a set repayment schedule. The principal and interest are paid monthly over the life of the loan.
- **Adjustable-Rate Loans**: In this structure, the interest rate changes over time based on market conditions, which can lead to lower payments initially but higher costs in the future.
- **Balloon Loans**: A balloon loan requires small payments over time with a large lump sum due at the end of the loan term. This type of loan can be a good option for those who plan to sell or refinance the property before the balloon payment comes due.
- **Secured Loans**: Many private lenders require that the loan be secured by the property being purchased. This means that if the borrower defaults, the lender can take possession of the property as collateral.

3.2 Key Loan Terms to Understand

When entering into a private loan agreement, understanding the following key terms is crucial:

- **Interest Rates**: Interest rates for private loans can vary significantly based on the lender, the borrower's risk profile, and the type of loan. Rates can be higher than traditional mortgages due to the increased risk for the lender.
- **Loan Term**: The loan term refers to how long the borrower has to repay the loan. It can range from a few months to several years, depending on the agreement.
- **Prepayment Penalties**: Some private loans may include penalties for paying off the loan early. Borrowers should check whether they can make early payments without facing additional fees.

3.3 Negotiating Loan Terms

Homebuyers have the ability to negotiate the terms of private loans, which is one of the advantages of working with private lenders. When negotiating, it's important to:

- Ensure that the loan terms are clear and reasonable.
- Compare interest rates with those of other private lenders or alternative financing methods.
- Discuss the possibility of refinancing the loan later, especially if the homebuyer plans to secure more traditional financing in the future.

Subsection 4: Assessing Risks and Protecting Your Investment

4.1 Risks of Peer-to-Peer Lending and Private Loans

While peer-to-peer lending and private loans offer flexible alternatives to traditional mortgages, they come with specific risks:

- **Higher Interest Rates**: Due to the perceived risk, private lenders may charge higher interest rates than banks, which can make the loan more expensive in the long term.
- **Default Risk**: If the borrower defaults on the loan, the lender may face challenges recouping their investment. Private loans are often less regulated than traditional loans, so protections may be limited.
- **Unclear Terms**: Unlike traditional mortgages, private loan agreements may not always have standardized terms, and some agreements could include hidden fees or unfavorable clauses for the borrower.

4.2 Protecting Your Investment

To protect your investment in a private loan, consider the following strategies:

- **Due Diligence**: Always conduct thorough research on the lender, the loan terms, and the property. Work with professionals (such as real estate agents or lawyers) who can help assess the deal.
- **Loan Agreement Review**: Have an attorney review the loan agreement to ensure all terms are fair and transparent.

How to Buy a House Without a Mortgage: Creative Financing Strategies

- **Loan Insurance**: Some private lenders offer insurance or protections against default. While this can increase upfront costs, it may offer valuable security in the event of financial difficulties.
- **Diversifying Risk**: If possible, consider spreading your investments across multiple loans to reduce the potential impact of a single loan default.

Conclusion

Peer-to-peer lending and private loans provide homebuyers with creative financing options that can be especially valuable for those who may not qualify for traditional mortgages. By understanding how these alternative financing methods work, finding the right lenders, structuring the loan agreement to suit your needs, and assessing risks, homebuyers can make informed decisions and protect their investment while achieving their dream of homeownership.

Chapter 11: Home Seller Donations and Gifts

Purchasing a home without a traditional mortgage can be an empowering option for many homebuyers, especially when utilizing creative financing strategies such as home seller donations or gifts. These approaches allow buyers to reduce or eliminate upfront costs and make homeownership more accessible. Seller donations and gifts provide an alternative method for obtaining funds for a down payment, closing costs, or other financial aspects of the purchase. This chapter explores how home seller donations and gifts work, the legal considerations involved, how to negotiate these contributions, and successful case studies of homebuyers who have used this strategy to purchase their homes.

Subsection 1: Understanding Seller Gifts or Donations

1.1 What are Seller Donations and Gifts?

A seller donation or gift occurs when the seller of a property agrees to contribute money or other forms of financial assistance towards the buyer's costs of purchasing the home. These contributions are typically applied to the buyer's down payment, closing costs, or in some cases, even towards reducing the principal balance of the home loan. The primary advantage for the buyer is that they can reduce the amount of money they need to bring to the table, making homeownership more achievable.

These gifts or donations are not common in all real estate transactions but can be found in specific market conditions or as part of a negotiated deal. Seller donations are particularly useful for buyers who may have difficulty securing enough cash upfront, especially first-time buyers, low-income buyers, or those purchasing in high-cost areas.

1.2 Types of Seller Gifts or Donations

How to Buy a House Without a Mortgage: Creative Financing Strategies

- **Down Payment Assistance**: Sellers may agree to contribute a certain amount toward the buyer's down payment, making it easier for the buyer to meet the down payment requirements for the home purchase.
- **Closing Cost Contributions**: Closing costs can be a significant expense for homebuyers, often amounting to thousands of dollars. Sellers may contribute a portion or all of the buyer's closing costs as part of the agreement.
- **Seller-Paid Points**: In some cases, sellers may agree to pay "points" on the buyer's loan, which can lower the interest rate over the life of the mortgage. Each point typically equals 1% of the loan amount.
- **Repairs and Improvements**: Instead of giving cash, the seller may offer to cover the cost of necessary repairs or improvements to the home, thus reducing the buyer's overall financial burden.

1.3 Why Sellers Offer Donations or Gifts

Sellers may offer these contributions as an incentive to attract buyers or to close a deal more quickly, especially in a competitive or slow real estate market. In some cases, offering a seller gift may be beneficial in helping the seller sell their home faster or at the desired price, especially if buyers have difficulty coming up with the funds for a down payment or closing costs. Seller donations can also be tax-deductible under specific circumstances, though this varies by jurisdiction and the exact nature of the donation.

Subsection 2: Legal Considerations for Seller Contributions

2.1 Legal Framework Surrounding Seller Gifts and Donations

While home seller donations or gifts are legal, there are important regulations and guidelines that both buyers and sellers must follow to ensure the transaction is legitimate. The following are key legal considerations to be aware of when negotiating or receiving a seller gift or donation:

- **Loan Program Restrictions**: Most loan programs have specific rules regarding seller contributions. For example, FHA and VA loans allow sellers to contribute to the buyer's closing costs or down payment, but there are limits based on the purchase price and loan type. Conventional loans also have caps on seller contributions, typically ranging from 3% to 9% of the purchase price, depending on the size of the down payment.
- **Gift vs. Loan**: The IRS treats a gift differently than a loan. For tax purposes, it is essential that the seller's contribution is considered a gift and not a loan. This means that the buyer should not be expected to repay the seller. If the seller's contribution is classified as a loan, it could have serious implications for both parties.
- **Documentation**: Proper documentation is required for seller gifts or donations. The buyer must often provide a "gift letter" that states the amount of the gift, the source of the funds, and that the gift is not a loan. The letter must also specify that the buyer is not expected to repay the gift. For certain loan types, additional forms or disclosures may be required to ensure that the donation is valid under the loan program's guidelines.
- **Lender Approval**: Lenders will typically review any seller contributions to ensure compliance with the terms of the loan. They may require documentation to verify the source of the gift, its amount, and that it meets their requirements.
- **Impact on Appraisal**: If a seller contributes too much toward the buyer's costs, the lender may require an appraisal to ensure that the home is worth the purchase price and that the loan amount is not inflated by the donation.

2.2 Tax Implications of Seller Donations

The tax implications of seller donations can vary depending on the amount of the gift and the nature of the transaction. Typically, the buyer does not have to pay taxes on a gift from the seller, as gifts are generally not taxable to the recipient. However, the seller may be subject to gift taxes if the amount exceeds the annual gift tax exclusion limit (currently around $15,000 per recipient). If the seller's donation exceeds this threshold, they may need to file a gift tax return.

It is essential that both parties consult with a tax professional to understand their specific tax responsibilities, especially for large gifts or donations. Additionally, if the donation is in the form of seller-paid points, there may be other tax considerations related to the mortgage.

Subsection 3: How to Negotiate a Seller Donation for Your Home

3.1 Initiating the Negotiation
When negotiating a seller donation, it's important to approach the discussion strategically:

- **Understand the Market**: Before you request a seller donation, understand the current real estate market. In a buyer's market, sellers may be more willing to offer contributions as they try to make their property stand out. In a seller's market, this request may be less successful unless there are specific circumstances (e.g., the property has been on the market for a long time).
- **Research Seller Motivation**: Sellers who are motivated to sell quickly may be more open to negotiations. For example, sellers who are relocating, dealing with a home that has been on the market for a while, or those who want to avoid a lengthy selling process may be more inclined to offer gifts or donations.

3.2 How to Make Your Case

- **Explain Your Financial Situation**: Clearly explain your financial situation to the seller and demonstrate why a seller

donation would make it easier for you to complete the purchase. Providing documentation showing your qualifications as a buyer but lacking the necessary funds for the down payment or closing costs can strengthen your case.
- **Offer a Fair Price**: If you're asking for a seller donation, make sure your offer is still competitive. Sellers may be more likely to agree to your request if they are still getting a fair price for the property.
- **Flexibility**: If the seller is unwilling to provide a full donation, consider negotiating for a smaller contribution or other forms of assistance, such as seller-paid closing costs or repairs.

3.3 Structuring the Donation

Be clear on how the seller's donation will be applied in the transaction. Whether it's for the down payment, closing costs, or reducing loan points, ensure both parties are clear on the terms of the donation. The specifics of how the donation is structured will need to be documented and submitted to the lender for approval, so clarity is crucial.

Subsection 4: Examples of Successful Home Purchases with Seller Donations

4.1 Case Study 1: First-Time Homebuyer Success

In a competitive housing market, a first-time homebuyer was struggling to come up with the down payment for a home they had found. After presenting their financial situation and expressing interest in a seller donation, the seller, motivated by the need to sell quickly, agreed to contribute 3% of the purchase price toward the buyer's closing costs. This allowed the buyer to secure financing for the property and close the deal.

4.2 Case Study 2: Negotiating Seller Contributions for Closing Costs

How to Buy a House Without a Mortgage: Creative Financing Strategies

A couple looking to purchase their first home was not able to cover both the down payment and closing costs. In negotiations with the seller, they asked for help with closing costs, and the seller agreed to contribute $5,000 towards those expenses. This arrangement allowed the buyers to complete the transaction without having to delay the purchase.

4.3 Case Study 3: Seller Gift for Home Improvement
In another scenario, a homebuyer agreed to purchase a property in need of significant repairs but lacked the cash to cover renovation costs. The seller, knowing the home would require substantial updates to make it livable, agreed to donate $10,000 toward the cost of repairs, effectively lowering the buyer's total out-of-pocket expenses.

Conclusion

Home seller donations and gifts are powerful, creative financing strategies that can make homeownership more accessible. By understanding how these donations work, the legal considerations involved, and how to negotiate a seller donation effectively, homebuyers can significantly reduce their upfront costs and move closer to homeownership without a traditional mortgage. With careful negotiation and understanding, both buyers and sellers can benefit from this unique financing option.

Chapter 12: Using Retirement Savings for Home Purchase

Using retirement savings to fund a home purchase can be an attractive option for many homebuyers who are looking for creative ways to finance their home without a traditional mortgage. With rising home prices, student loan debts, and other financial obligations, tapping into retirement savings can offer the necessary funds to help make homeownership a reality. This chapter provides a comprehensive guide to understanding the process of using retirement savings, particularly 401(k)s and IRAs, for home purchase, exploring the rules, regulations, benefits, and drawbacks of this method.

Subsection 1: Tapping into Your Retirement Accounts

1.1 What is Tapping into Retirement Savings?
Tapping into retirement savings refers to using funds from retirement accounts such as a 401(k) or an Individual Retirement Account (IRA) to cover a home purchase. This can be a way to secure the upfront capital needed for a down payment, closing costs, or even the entire purchase, depending on the type of account and the amount available. While these accounts are primarily designed for long-term retirement savings, certain provisions allow individuals to withdraw or borrow money to buy a home, making it a viable option for creative home financing.

1.2 Types of Retirement Accounts for Home Purchase

- **401(k) Accounts**: A 401(k) is an employer-sponsored retirement plan that allows employees to contribute a portion of their income before taxes. Some 401(k) plans offer the option to take out a loan or a hardship withdrawal for the purpose of purchasing a home. The amount you can borrow typically ranges from 50% of your vested balance, up to a maximum of $50,000.

How to Buy a House Without a Mortgage: Creative Financing Strategies

- **Individual Retirement Accounts (IRA)**: An IRA is an individual account that can be opened independently, allowing for tax-advantaged growth. There are two main types: Traditional IRAs and Roth IRAs. While these accounts are primarily used for retirement savings, they can be used to purchase a home under specific conditions, with different rules for each type.

1.3 Using Retirement Savings for Down Payments or Full Purchase

- **Down Payment**: Many homebuyers use their retirement savings for the down payment, which can be one of the largest financial hurdles to overcome when purchasing a home. Using 401(k) funds or IRA distributions can help meet this critical need.
- **Full Home Purchase**: In rare cases, a buyer may have enough in their retirement accounts to purchase a home outright, though this is more common for individuals who have significant savings in their retirement plans.

Subsection 2: Rules and Regulations on Using 401(k)s or IRAs for Real Estate

2.1 Rules for 401(k) Withdrawals or Loans for Home Purchase

- **401(k) Loan**: Many 401(k) plans allow you to borrow money from your retirement account, typically up to 50% of your vested balance, or a maximum of $50,000. The loan is repaid with interest over a period of time, usually five years. This can be a viable option for a home purchase, as the interest you pay goes back into your 401(k) account. However, if you leave your job while you still have an outstanding loan, the balance may need to be repaid in full, or it could be considered a taxable distribution.

- **401(k) Hardship Withdrawal**: A hardship withdrawal allows you to take money from your 401(k) for specific reasons, including purchasing a primary residence. The withdrawal is subject to income tax, and individuals under 59 ½ years old are generally subject to a 10% early withdrawal penalty, though this penalty may be waived under certain conditions.

2.2 Rules for IRA Withdrawals for Home Purchase

- **Traditional IRA**: A Traditional IRA allows individuals to withdraw up to $10,000 without penalty for the purchase of a first home, provided the funds are used for the purchase within 120 days of the withdrawal. However, you will still need to pay income tax on the amount withdrawn, as Traditional IRA funds are tax-deferred.
- **Roth IRA**: With a Roth IRA, you can withdraw your contributions at any time, tax- and penalty-free, because you've already paid taxes on that money. For earnings, you may withdraw up to $10,000 for the purchase of a first home, and if you've had the Roth IRA open for at least five years, the earnings will be tax-free as well. However, if you withdraw earnings before five years or use the money for something other than a first-time home purchase, you may be subject to taxes and penalties.

2.3 Special Considerations for First-Time Homebuyers

The IRS defines a first-time homebuyer as someone who has not owned a home in the past two years. This definition allows homebuyers to take advantage of certain withdrawal benefits, such as the $10,000 penalty-free withdrawal from an IRA for a first home purchase. This rule applies to both Traditional and Roth IRAs, though it is subject to specific conditions.

Subsection 3: Pros and Cons of Using Retirement Savings

How to Buy a House Without a Mortgage: Creative Financing Strategies

3.1 Pros of Using Retirement Savings for Home Purchase

- **Accessibility of Funds**: If you're struggling to gather enough funds for a down payment or closing costs, tapping into your retirement savings may provide a quick solution.
- **Avoid Mortgage Qualification**: Using retirement funds can help you avoid traditional mortgage qualification processes, which can be difficult for some buyers, especially those with less-than-ideal credit.
- **No Monthly Payments**: If you choose to withdraw money from your retirement account or take a loan with favorable terms, you can avoid the monthly mortgage payments associated with traditional financing methods.
- **Tax Advantages**: Certain IRAs, like Roth IRAs, offer tax-free withdrawals for first-time home purchases, which can be a significant advantage.

3.2 Cons of Using Retirement Savings for Home Purchase

- **Risk to Retirement Security**: By withdrawing or borrowing money from your retirement accounts, you risk jeopardizing your long-term financial security. These funds are meant to sustain you during retirement, and using them for a home purchase can leave you with less money for your future.
- **Early Withdrawal Penalties**: If you're under 59 ½, early withdrawal penalties (usually 10%) and taxes can diminish the amount you receive from your retirement account, which may make it a costly decision.
- **Loan Repayment Terms**: If you take a loan from your 401(k), you'll need to repay the loan with interest. If you fail to repay the loan, the balance may be treated as taxable income, and you could also face penalties.
- **Potential Impact on Retirement Growth**: Withdrawing money from your retirement account can decrease the potential growth of your funds due to the loss of compound interest, thus impacting your financial future.

Subsection 4: How to Minimize Penalties and Maximize Benefits

4.1 Strategies for Minimizing Penalties

- **Use the Funds for a First-Time Home Purchase**: Take advantage of the specific provisions for first-time homebuyers in both 401(k) and IRA accounts. This can help you avoid early withdrawal penalties.
- **Plan Your Withdrawal Timing**: If you are under 59 ½ and must make an early withdrawal, consider carefully timing your withdrawals to minimize the impact of penalties. If possible, utilize the 401(k) loan option, as loans are not subject to penalties.
- **Consult a Financial Advisor**: Before making any withdrawal or loan, consult a financial advisor to fully understand the tax implications and how the withdrawal will impact your retirement goals.

4.2 Maximizing the Benefits of Using Retirement Savings

- **Consider Loan Repayment Terms**: If you decide to take a loan from your 401(k), ensure that you can comfortably repay it within the stipulated terms. This will help prevent negative consequences such as additional taxes and penalties.
- **Use Roth IRA Contributions**: If you have a Roth IRA, consider using your contributions, as they are tax- and penalty-free. Additionally, if you've had the Roth IRA for more than five years, you can use the earnings as well, without penalty.
- **Strategize Your Home Purchase**: If you're planning to use retirement savings for your home purchase, make sure it aligns with your long-term financial goals. Ensure that you're not jeopardizing your retirement savings for short-term gain.

How to Buy a House Without a Mortgage: Creative Financing Strategies

Conclusion

Using retirement savings to purchase a home can be a strategic move to make homeownership possible, especially when traditional mortgage financing is not an option. However, it's essential to carefully understand the rules and regulations surrounding 401(k) and IRA withdrawals, as well as the pros and cons associated with tapping into your retirement funds. By weighing the benefits against the risks, and consulting a financial advisor, you can make an informed decision that helps you achieve homeownership while safeguarding your retirement future.

How to Buy a House Without a Mortgage: Creative Financing Strategies

Chapter 13: Sweat Equity and Building Your Home

In the realm of creative home financing, sweat equity stands out as a valuable tool for those looking to build or improve their homes without relying on a traditional mortgage. Sweat equity refers to the labor and effort put into a project, whether it's building a house from the ground up or renovating an existing property, which can increase the value of the home. In this chapter, we will delve into how sweat equity works, how it can be applied to homeownership, and how individuals can leverage it to build or purchase their dream homes without the burden of a conventional mortgage. This chapter will cover the essential concepts, strategies, and techniques to help you get the most out of your sweat equity investment.

Subsection 1: What is Sweat Equity?

1.1 Definition of Sweat Equity

Sweat equity is the value added to a property or project through the physical effort and labor of an individual or team, rather than through financial investment. In the context of homeownership, it refers to the work you put into building or improving a house, which increases its overall value. This concept is particularly appealing for homebuyers and investors who have the skills and time to undertake projects themselves rather than relying solely on professional labor or taking out large loans.

1.2 Types of Sweat Equity in Homeownership

- **Home Building**: Building a home from scratch, whether it is a custom home or using a kit, requires significant labor and expertise. This process involves land clearing, foundation work, framing, plumbing, electrical, and finishing touches. The sweat equity comes from completing much of the work yourself, which can save substantial costs compared to hiring contractors.

- **Renovation**: Renovating an existing property is another popular way to build sweat equity. Tasks can range from minor cosmetic improvements, like painting and landscaping, to more extensive remodels, such as kitchen or bathroom upgrades, flooring installation, or structural repairs.

1.3 Benefits of Sweat Equity

- **Cost Savings**: The most significant benefit of sweat equity is the money you save by doing the work yourself. By avoiding contractor fees and using your labor, you reduce the overall cost of the project.
- **Increased Property Value**: By adding physical value to the property, you can increase its market price. A well-executed renovation or new build often leads to a higher property value, giving you a return on your time and effort.
- **Sense of Accomplishment**: Building or renovating a home offers the satisfaction of creating something with your hands and seeing the results of your hard work.

Subsection 2: How to Build Equity Through Home Renovation

2.1 Understanding Home Renovation and Equity Building

Home renovation is one of the most common ways homeowners build equity through sweat equity. Renovation projects can improve both the aesthetic and functional aspects of a home, increasing its appeal to potential buyers or lenders. While some renovations might not offer a high return on investment (ROI), others, such as kitchen remodels or energy-efficient improvements, can substantially boost a property's value.

2.2 Key Renovation Projects to Build Sweat Equity

- **Kitchen and Bathroom Remodels**: These are often the highest-return renovations, as they directly impact the

livability and desirability of a home. Simple changes like replacing cabinets, updating fixtures, or installing new countertops can significantly enhance the home's value.
- **Adding Square Footage**: Increasing the square footage of a home by finishing a basement, adding an extra bedroom, or expanding the living area is an excellent way to increase value. Expanding usable space allows homeowners to raise the asking price without necessarily increasing construction costs.
- **Curb Appeal Improvements**: Landscaping, exterior painting, or new siding can dramatically improve first impressions and increase a home's resale value. Curb appeal is essential in attracting potential buyers and can be a cost-effective way to build equity.
- **Energy-Efficient Upgrades**: Installing energy-efficient windows, solar panels, or insulation may require an upfront investment, but these improvements can lead to long-term savings and a higher home valuation.

2.3 Assessing ROI of Renovation Projects

To ensure you're getting the most out of your sweat equity, it's essential to prioritize renovations that offer a high return on investment. Research local market trends and consult with a real estate agent or appraiser to determine which improvements are most likely to increase your home's value.

Subsection 3: Contracting and DIY Homebuilding

3.1 Contracting Your Project

For many, the thought of building a home or undertaking a significant renovation project can seem daunting. While DIY projects can save money, some aspects of homebuilding and renovations may require the skills of specialized contractors. Contractors can assist with areas like electrical work, plumbing, or structural engineering. Understanding when to hire a professional and when to take on a project yourself is critical for maximizing your sweat equity.

- **General Contractor**: A general contractor can oversee the entire project, managing various subcontractors (plumbers, electricians, etc.) and ensuring that the work complies with local regulations and building codes. Hiring a general contractor might cost more upfront, but it ensures the quality and speed of the project.
- **Subcontractors**: If you prefer to take on the role of project manager yourself, you can hire individual subcontractors to handle specific tasks, such as drywall installation or roofing. This can save money but requires significant time management and knowledge of construction processes.

3.2 DIY Homebuilding

If you have the skills, knowledge, and time, DIY homebuilding can be a rewarding way to create sweat equity. Whether it's building a small cabin or constructing a larger home, there are a few key considerations:

- **Pre-Construction Planning**: Understand the necessary permits and regulations for building a home. Developing a detailed plan, including blueprints, budgeting, and timelines, is crucial for ensuring the project runs smoothly.
- **Learning the Basics**: There are many resources available online, including tutorials and instructional videos, to help guide you through various aspects of construction, from framing to roofing. Acquiring the necessary skills beforehand will help reduce mistakes and inefficiencies.
- **Building a Team**: While it's possible to build a home entirely on your own, it may be wise to recruit skilled friends or hire part-time laborers to assist with the heavy lifting.

3.3 Challenges and Rewards of DIY Homebuilding

- **Time Commitment**: DIY homebuilding is a significant time commitment and may take longer than hiring a contractor. However, the reward is having a home built according to your specifications, with the added benefit of equity creation.

- **Physical Demands**: Homebuilding can be physically demanding. Make sure you're prepared for the labor involved and have the necessary tools and equipment to handle the tasks at hand.

Subsection 4: How Sweat Equity Affects Property Value

4.1 Impact of Sweat Equity on Market Value
The money invested in sweat equity generally adds more value to a property than simply spending on materials and labor. Sweat equity reflects the personal effort and skill used to improve the property, which in turn, can make it more attractive to potential buyers. Renovations and improvements that increase functionality or aesthetic appeal often lead to higher appraisal values.

4.2 Market Trends and Appraisals
The impact of sweat equity on property value can depend on local market trends. In some markets, buyers may prioritize modernized kitchens or spacious, energy-efficient homes. In others, the added equity from sweat may not be as easily recognized unless it's accompanied by professional appraisals and real estate agent support.

4.3 Maximizing Sweat Equity Value
To ensure that your sweat equity results in a significant increase in property value, it's essential to focus on the projects that have the most considerable impact on your home's functionality and aesthetic appeal. Quality workmanship and attention to detail will also ensure that potential buyers or appraisers recognize the value you've added.

Conclusion

Sweat equity is a powerful tool in the world of homeownership. By putting in the physical effort to build or renovate a home, individuals

How to Buy a House Without a Mortgage: Creative Financing Strategies

can significantly reduce costs, increase property value, and create a more personalized living space. However, to truly leverage sweat equity for homeownership, it's essential to understand which projects provide the highest return, when to hire professionals, and how to maximize the overall value of your property. Whether you're building a home from scratch or renovating an existing one, sweat equity can make homeownership attainable without the burden of a traditional mortgage.

Chapter 14: Government and Non-Profit Financing Programs

In the pursuit of homeownership without a traditional mortgage, government programs and non-profit organizations offer an invaluable set of resources that can significantly reduce the financial burden of buying a home. This chapter will explore the various government and non-profit financing programs available, how to navigate them, and how to take advantage of these opportunities to purchase a home without taking on a conventional mortgage.

Government and non-profit financing programs are designed to make homeownership more accessible, especially for first-time homebuyers, low-income families, and individuals facing challenges in securing financing from traditional lenders. These programs often offer lower interest rates, down payment assistance, and other benefits, making it easier to achieve debt-free homeownership.

Subsection 1: Available Government Programs for First-Time Homebuyers

1.1 Overview of Government Programs

Government programs for first-time homebuyers are designed to promote affordable housing by offering financial assistance, lower down payments, and reduced interest rates. These programs vary by country and region but generally focus on helping people who may struggle to qualify for conventional mortgages. Some of the most common government-backed programs for first-time homebuyers include:

- **FHA Loans (Federal Housing Administration Loans)**: In the U.S., FHA loans are a popular government-backed mortgage program aimed at helping low-to-moderate-income first-time buyers. They require a smaller down payment (as low as 3.5%) and are easier to qualify for compared to

conventional loans. FHA loans are available through approved lenders and offer lower interest rates.
- **VA Loans (Veterans Affairs Loans)**: VA loans are available to U.S. military veterans, active-duty service members, and their families. These loans offer significant advantages, including no down payment requirements and competitive interest rates. VA loans do not require mortgage insurance, making them a highly favorable option for eligible buyers.
- **USDA Loans (United States Department of Agriculture Loans)**: These loans are designed to assist buyers in rural and suburban areas. USDA loans offer 100% financing, meaning no down payment is required, and they are available to individuals with low to moderate incomes. These loans are issued by approved lenders but are backed by the U.S. Department of Agriculture.
- **First-Time Homebuyer Grants and Down Payment Assistance**: Many local, state, and federal government programs provide financial assistance in the form of grants, down payment assistance, and subsidies. These programs help first-time buyers reduce upfront costs and make homeownership more attainable.

1.2 Key Features of Government Programs

- **Lower Down Payments**: Many government programs offer reduced or no down payment requirements, making homeownership more accessible.
- **Lower Interest Rates**: Government-backed loans often come with lower interest rates than conventional loans, reducing the overall cost of homeownership.
- **Flexible Credit Requirements**: Some programs are more lenient regarding credit score requirements, offering more opportunities for individuals who might not qualify for traditional loans.

1.3 Eligibility Criteria for Government Programs
To qualify for these programs, homebuyers typically need to meet

certain income limits, purchase a property in an eligible area, and be a first-time homebuyer. Other factors, such as employment history and credit score, may also be considered.

Subsection 2: Non-Profit Organizations Supporting Debt-Free Homeownership

2.1 Overview of Non-Profit Homeownership Programs
Several non-profit organizations focus on helping individuals achieve homeownership without the burden of a traditional mortgage. These organizations often provide down payment assistance, homebuyer education programs, and low-cost financing options. Some of the most prominent non-profit organizations involved in debt-free homeownership include:

- **Habitat for Humanity**: Habitat for Humanity is a global non-profit organization that helps families build and buy affordable homes. In many cases, Habitat offers homes with zero-interest loans or extremely low-interest loans, and in some cases, no mortgage is required. Habitat homeowners are also required to contribute "sweat equity," which means participating in the construction of their homes.
- **Local Non-Profit Housing Assistance Programs**: Many communities have local non-profit organizations dedicated to providing affordable housing options. These programs may offer assistance with down payments, housing counseling, or help with negotiating favorable loan terms. These programs vary by region, but they all aim to provide more accessible pathways to homeownership for low- and moderate-income families.

2.2 Benefits of Non-Profit Homeownership Programs

- **No or Low-Interest Loans**: Non-profit organizations often offer interest-free or low-interest loans, which significantly

reduce the cost of homeownership and help individuals avoid traditional mortgage debt.
- **Down Payment Assistance**: Many non-profits provide down payment assistance, which can help buyers cover the upfront costs of purchasing a home.
- **Homebuyer Education**: Non-profit organizations often offer homebuyer education workshops that teach individuals the basics of budgeting, saving for a home, and understanding the homebuying process.

2.3 How to Find Non-Profit Programs

- **Community Outreach**: Local non-profit organizations often work closely with community groups, churches, and schools. Reaching out to these organizations can provide insight into available programs.
- **State and Local Housing Agencies**: State and local housing agencies often partner with non-profits to provide affordable housing programs. Contacting these agencies can help individuals find resources in their area.

Subsection 3: Navigating Financial Assistance and Subsidies

3.1 Understanding Financial Assistance Options
Financial assistance programs and subsidies can help reduce the financial burden of homeownership by covering some or all of the down payment and closing costs. Government and non-profit organizations provide various forms of assistance, including:

- **Grants**: These are funds that do not need to be repaid and are typically used to cover down payments or closing costs. Many first-time homebuyer programs offer grants to help buyers get started.
- **Subsidized Loans**: These are loans offered at reduced interest rates, often below the market rate, to help buyers

afford homeownership. Some programs offer deferred interest, which means no payments are required until the home is sold.
- **Down Payment Assistance**: Some programs provide funds specifically for down payments. These funds may be offered as grants, low-interest loans, or forgivable loans (where the loan is forgiven if the buyer remains in the home for a specified number of years).

3.2 How to Qualify for Financial Assistance
Qualifying for financial assistance usually requires meeting certain criteria, such as being a first-time homebuyer, meeting income limits, and purchasing a home within an approved price range. Each program has specific requirements that must be met to ensure eligibility. In some cases, buyers may also need to attend homebuyer education courses to qualify for assistance.

3.3 Finding Financial Assistance Programs

- **State Housing Agencies**: State housing agencies are a key source of financial assistance programs. These agencies often administer federal funds and provide details about local programs.
- **Online Resources**: Many online platforms and government websites provide searchable databases of financial assistance programs. Websites like the U.S. Department of Housing and Urban Development (HUD) offer tools to help homebuyers locate programs in their area.

Subsection 4: How to Apply and Qualify for Government-Backed Programs

4.1 The Application Process
The application process for government-backed programs generally involves several steps, including:

How to Buy a House Without a Mortgage: Creative Financing Strategies

- **Researching Available Programs**: The first step is to research the available programs that suit your needs and location. Local, state, and federal programs may have different eligibility requirements and benefits.
- **Gathering Documentation**: Once you've identified a program, you'll need to gather required documentation, including proof of income, employment history, credit score, and personal identification. Each program has different documentation requirements.
- **Submitting the Application**: After gathering your documents, you'll submit an application through the program's website or by working directly with an approved lender or housing agency.

4.2 Meeting Eligibility Criteria
To qualify for government-backed programs, you typically need to meet specific criteria, such as:

- Being a first-time homebuyer (in most cases)
- Having a household income below a certain threshold
- Purchasing a home in a designated area (such as a rural or underserved area)
- Maintaining a minimum credit score

4.3 Working with a Housing Counselor
Many government programs require or recommend that applicants work with a certified housing counselor. Housing counselors can help guide you through the application process, explain the details of different programs, and provide advice on how to manage finances.

4.4 Tips for Improving Your Chances of Approval

- **Improve Your Credit Score**: A higher credit score increases your chances of qualifying for government-backed programs. Make sure to review your credit report and address any issues before applying.

- **Reduce Debt**: Reducing your debt-to-income ratio (DTI) can also improve your chances of approval.
- **Save for a Down Payment**: While some programs offer down payment assistance, having some savings set aside can make your application more appealing.

Conclusion

Government and non-profit financing programs provide valuable opportunities for those looking to purchase a home without relying on a traditional mortgage. By leveraging these resources, homebuyers can access affordable loans, down payment assistance, and educational programs that make homeownership more attainable. Whether you are a first-time homebuyer or someone looking for alternative financing, government and non-profit programs offer a range of options to help you achieve your dream of homeownership without the burden of a traditional mortgage.

How to Buy a House Without a Mortgage: Creative Financing Strategies

Chapter 15: Borrowing From Family and Friends

One of the most innovative ways to buy a house without a traditional mortgage is by borrowing from family members or friends. This form of financing, often referred to as "peer lending" or "informal loans," can provide much-needed capital for purchasing a home without going through banks or other financial institutions. However, borrowing money from loved ones can come with its own unique set of challenges, risks, and responsibilities.

In this chapter, we will delve into how borrowing from family and friends can be a viable strategy for homebuyers who wish to avoid traditional mortgages. We will explore how to structure these loans, the dos and don'ts of borrowing from loved ones, how to maintain healthy financial relationships, and the legal implications of such loans.

Subsection 1: Structuring a Loan Agreement with Friends or Family

1.1 Why Formalize the Loan Agreement?
Borrowing from family or friends may seem like an easy and informal arrangement, but it's important to treat the agreement with the same seriousness and professionalism as you would a loan from a bank. A formalized loan agreement protects both parties—ensuring that expectations are clear, the repayment plan is well-defined, and potential misunderstandings are minimized.

A well-structured loan agreement outlines the following key elements:

- **Loan Amount**: Specify the total amount of money being borrowed. Be clear about whether it is a lump sum or multiple installments.
- **Interest Rate**: While family and friends may offer loans with little or no interest, it's important to decide on an interest rate

or clarify if the loan is interest-free. The IRS requires that a minimum interest rate be charged on loans between family members to avoid tax implications.
- **Repayment Terms**: Clearly outline how and when the loan will be repaid. This includes monthly payments, lump sum payments, or a timeline for the loan's full repayment. Be realistic about your financial situation and set a reasonable repayment schedule.
- **Collateral**: If you are using the loan to purchase property, it's wise to discuss whether the loan will be secured or unsecured. If secured, the property can act as collateral, which means the lender could potentially take possession of it if the borrower defaults.
- **Default Conditions**: Define what happens if you fail to make the payments as agreed. Will there be penalties, or is there a provision for renegotiating the terms? This is crucial to avoid any misunderstandings down the line.

1.2 Drafting a Written Agreement

Although verbal agreements may be sufficient in some informal situations, having a written loan agreement offers clarity and legal protection for both the borrower and the lender. It is advisable to seek legal counsel to draft or review the agreement. Legal professionals can ensure that the loan is properly documented and complies with tax and legal regulations.

A well-crafted loan agreement might include:

- The full names of both the borrower and the lender.
- The loan amount and the agreed interest rate (if applicable).
- The terms of repayment (e.g., installment amounts, due dates, and final payment).
- Collateral arrangements (if any).
- Default clauses and consequences.

How to Buy a House Without a Mortgage: Creative Financing Strategies

A written loan agreement ensures that both parties know their responsibilities and can refer to the terms in case of any future disputes.

Subsection 2: The Dos and Don'ts of Borrowing from Loved Ones

2.1 The Dos of Borrowing from Family and Friends

- **Do Be Transparent**: Clear communication is key to a successful loan agreement. Be upfront with your family and friends about your financial situation, your plans to repay the loan, and any potential risks involved.
- **Do Treat It Like a Business Deal**: Just because the loan is between family or friends doesn't mean it should be treated casually. The loan should be handled with professionalism, with a formal agreement and clear repayment terms.
- **Do Involve Legal Professionals**: Even though the loan is informal, consulting a lawyer to create the loan agreement can help ensure it's legally sound and that both parties are protected.
- **Do Plan for Contingencies**: Life circumstances change, and so should your repayment plan. Make sure that both parties are clear on what happens if something unexpected happens, like loss of income, illness, or the need to extend the loan term.

2.2 The Don'ts of Borrowing from Family and Friends

- **Don't Borrow More Than You Can Repay**: It's easy to get carried away when borrowing from family and friends, especially if they are offering help. However, only borrow what you can realistically repay, even if there are no formal payments due immediately.

- **Don't Make It Emotional**: Money can create tensions in relationships. Avoid letting emotions cloud your judgment, and remember that this is a financial transaction, not a favor or gift. Keeping it professional helps maintain healthy relationships.
- **Don't Ignore Tax Implications**: Loans between family and friends have tax implications. The IRS requires that a minimum interest rate be charged on loans over a certain amount, even between family members, to prevent the transaction from being seen as a gift. Failing to comply with tax rules can result in penalties or back taxes.
- **Don't Overlook Documentation**: Even though the lender is a friend or family member, not having written documentation of the loan can lead to confusion or misunderstandings later. Always ensure that the agreement is clearly documented and signed by both parties.

Subsection 3: How to Ensure a Healthy Financial Relationship

3.1 Keep Communication Open

One of the most important elements of borrowing from loved ones is maintaining open lines of communication. If you experience financial difficulty or anticipate delays in repayment, communicate this early on. Being transparent about your financial situation and intentions will help prevent misunderstandings and hurt feelings.

Regular updates about your financial situation and progress with the loan can also help both parties feel more comfortable and secure in the arrangement.

3.2 Treating the Loan Like a Business Transaction

To avoid potential strains on relationships, treat the loan as a formal, business transaction. Make sure both parties know the terms and conditions and are clear about what is expected. Be punctual with

How to Buy a House Without a Mortgage: Creative Financing Strategies

payments and try to avoid any informal adjustments to the terms without first consulting the lender.

3.3 Avoid Mixing Personal and Financial Matters
While it's natural for the borrower to feel grateful or indebted, it's important to separate personal feelings from financial obligations. Doing so helps to maintain a healthy financial relationship. Ensure that the borrower and lender can still enjoy a personal relationship without financial matters overshadowing it.

3.4 Consider the Long-Term Impact
Even if the relationship is strong and positive, borrowing money from loved ones can change the dynamic of the relationship. If problems arise—whether in repaying the loan or misunderstandings about the terms—it can cause resentment or emotional strain. Keep in mind that the long-term success of both the loan agreement and the relationship depends on handling the arrangement professionally and respectfully.

Subsection 4: Repayment Plans and Legal Considerations

4.1 Establishing a Realistic Repayment Plan
The repayment plan should be based on the borrower's financial capacity. Whether it involves monthly payments or lump sums, it's essential that the repayment terms are feasible and realistic. Create a payment plan that reflects the borrower's ability to make timely payments without putting undue stress on their finances.

4.2 Types of Repayment Arrangements

- **Fixed Payments**: These are regular, consistent payments over a set period of time.
- **Flexible Payments**: Some arrangements allow for flexibility in repayment, with amounts adjusted depending on the borrower's income or financial situation.

- **Balloon Payments**: This structure allows for smaller monthly payments and a lump sum payment at the end of the loan term.

4.3 Legal Considerations When Borrowing from Family and Friends

While borrowing money from family or friends is informal, it still involves legal considerations:

- **Tax Implications**: If the loan amount exceeds certain thresholds, it may be subject to taxation. Loans from family members may be seen as taxable gifts unless the correct interest rate is charged, according to IRS guidelines. It's essential to understand the gift tax rules and the proper documentation required for the transaction.
- **Gift Tax**: In cases where the loan is not repaid, the IRS may consider the loan to be a gift. This could result in gift tax liabilities if the loan amount exceeds the annual gift tax exclusion.
- **Legal Recourse**: In cases of default, the lender may have legal recourse to pursue repayment through a court system, even if the loan is informal. Having a clear loan agreement will help the lender in these cases.

4.4 Renegotiating Loan Terms

Life circumstances can change, and renegotiating the loan terms may be necessary if the borrower is unable to meet the original repayment plan. It's essential to approach renegotiation respectfully and with clear communication. Any new terms should be documented in a revised loan agreement.

Conclusion

Borrowing from family and friends can be a powerful way to finance a home without relying on traditional mortgage institutions.

107 How to Buy a House Without a Mortgage: Creative Financing Strategies

However, it requires careful planning, clear communication, and a formal agreement to ensure that the financial arrangement doesn't strain relationships. By structuring the loan properly, maintaining professionalism, and adhering to legal and tax considerations, you can minimize the risks and successfully use family or friend loans to secure your dream home.

How to Buy a House Without a Mortgage: Creative Financing Strategies

Chapter 16: Purchasing a Property with a Business Partner

Purchasing a property without a traditional mortgage is a creative, strategic approach that many homebuyers explore when they are seeking alternatives to financing. One such method is to partner with a business partner for the purchase of real estate. Whether for personal or investment purposes, co-ownership can offer numerous advantages, such as shared financial burden, access to better properties, and enhanced buying power. However, it comes with its own complexities, risks, and considerations that need to be carefully planned and structured.

In this chapter, we will delve into the concept of purchasing property with a business partner, exploring the fundamentals of co-ownership, the importance of drafting a legal partnership agreement, how to manage shared ownership, and the strategies for exiting the partnership should the need arise.

Subsection 1: Co-Ownership and Business Partnerships for Home Purchase

1.1 What is Co-Ownership?
Co-ownership refers to the situation where two or more individuals share the ownership of a property. In the context of home buying, co-ownership is typically structured as a partnership between individuals who pool their resources (financial and otherwise) to purchase a home or investment property. This allows both parties to benefit from the property's value appreciation, rental income, or other financial advantages.

Co-ownership can take several forms:

- **Joint Tenancy**: All parties have equal ownership and rights to the property. If one co-owner dies, their share automatically transfers to the surviving co-owner(s).

How to Buy a House Without a Mortgage: Creative Financing Strategies

- **Tenancy in Common**: Each party owns a specific share of the property, which may be equal or unequal. In this arrangement, each co-owner's share can be sold, transferred, or passed down to heirs.
- **Limited Liability Companies (LLC)**: Some partners may choose to create an LLC for the purpose of owning and managing the property. This protects the individuals' personal assets while giving them flexibility in terms of property management and taxation.

Co-ownership works well in scenarios where both parties have complementary goals and resources. This might include:

- **Homebuyers with Limited Capital**: Two or more individuals who wish to buy a property together but lack sufficient funds to purchase a property independently.
- **Investment Property**: Partners may decide to invest in real estate together, with the goal of generating rental income or flipping properties for profit.
- **Family or Friends**: Individuals may decide to co-own a property for personal reasons, such as purchasing a second home, vacation property, or living together in the same home.

1.2 Benefits of Co-Ownership in Home Buying

The primary benefits of co-owning a property with a business partner include:

- **Increased Buying Power**: Pooling financial resources allows both parties to afford a higher-value property than they could on their own.
- **Shared Risk**: The financial burden of homeownership, including mortgage payments, property taxes, maintenance costs, and other expenses, is shared between the partners, reducing the individual's financial risk.
- **Diversified Investment**: Co-owning property with a partner can provide access to real estate investment opportunities

that may have been otherwise out of reach for either party individually.

However, there are also challenges that come with co-owning a property, including disagreements over management and maintenance, unequal contributions, and different long-term goals.

Subsection 2: Drawing Up a Legal Partnership Agreement

2.1 Importance of a Legal Partnership Agreement

While co-ownership can be an exciting way to invest in real estate or purchase a home, it is critical to draft a detailed legal partnership agreement that sets clear terms and expectations for the partnership. This agreement will act as a binding document that outlines the rights, responsibilities, and obligations of each co-owner.

The agreement should address several key elements, including:

- **Ownership Shares**: The document should specify the percentage of ownership for each party. These shares can be equal or reflect the individual contributions made by each party (e.g., one party contributes more capital than the other).
- **Financial Contributions**: Clearly outline how much each party will contribute to the purchase price, closing costs, and ongoing expenses such as mortgage payments, insurance, and maintenance costs. This will help prevent misunderstandings down the line.
- **Decision-Making Process**: A clear process for decision-making must be established. Decisions regarding property management, maintenance, repairs, and any future sale or refinance should be outlined. Will all decisions require unanimous approval, or will a majority vote suffice?
- **Dispute Resolution**: The agreement should include procedures for resolving conflicts. This might involve

mediation or arbitration to prevent issues from escalating to litigation.
- **Exit Strategy**: The partnership agreement should also define how to handle situations where one co-owner wants to sell their share or exit the partnership entirely.

2.2 Key Components of the Partnership Agreement

- **Roles and Responsibilities**: Establish clear roles, including who is responsible for the day-to-day management of the property, paying bills, and handling maintenance.
- **Financing Terms**: Include terms relating to financing, such as how each party's share of the mortgage will be handled, whether there will be joint or separate accounts for payment, and how the loan is secured.
- **Property Use and Occupancy**: If the property is being co-purchased for residential use, the agreement should clarify the living arrangements, including how space will be divided and any use restrictions.
- **Exit Clauses**: Clearly define the process for one partner selling their share, buying out the other partner, or selling the property entirely. The exit strategy should include a mechanism for determining the property's market value at the time of sale, and how proceeds will be divided.

Subsection 3: Managing Shared Ownership of Real Estate

3.1 Effective Communication Between Co-Owners
Clear and consistent communication is vital for managing shared ownership. Regular check-ins and updates on the property's condition, financial obligations, and future plans can help ensure that both parties are aligned and any concerns are addressed early. This is particularly important when it comes to decisions about property improvements, repairs, and addressing tenant or maintenance issues.

3.2 Property Management Roles

In some cases, one co-owner may take on a more active role in managing the property, especially if it is an investment property or rental. In these cases, the co-owner assuming the property management role should be compensated for their time and effort, as agreed upon in the partnership agreement. Alternatively, co-owners can hire a professional property manager to handle the day-to-day responsibilities, which can save time but will require additional costs.

3.3 Financial Responsibilities

It is essential that both co-owners remain diligent in fulfilling their financial responsibilities. Each party should ensure they are contributing their agreed share toward monthly mortgage payments, utilities, property taxes, insurance, and maintenance costs. If one co-owner fails to pay their share, it can lead to tensions and even legal disputes. Setting up a joint account specifically for property expenses can help manage these obligations.

Subsection 4: Exit Strategies and Protection for Co-Owners

4.1 Planning for the Unexpected

While co-owning a property can be a mutually beneficial arrangement, it is important to plan for situations where one or both co-owners may want to exit the partnership. This may happen due to a change in personal circumstances, a shift in financial goals, or simply a desire to sell the property.

4.2 Buyout Clauses

One of the most important provisions in a co-ownership agreement is the buyout clause. This outlines how a co-owner can buy out the other's share of the property if they wish to exit the partnership. The clause should include:

- **Valuation Process**: How the property's market value will be determined at the time of buyout.

- **Payment Terms**: How the buyout will be financed (lump sum or installments).
- **Timeframe**: A timeline for completing the buyout.

4.3 Selling the Property
In some cases, both co-owners may agree that selling the property is the best option. The agreement should specify how the property will be sold, how proceeds will be divided, and what steps will be taken in the event of disagreement over the sale.

4.4 Exit Strategy for Death or Disability
The partnership agreement should also account for scenarios where one co-owner dies or becomes disabled and is no longer able to manage or participate in the property. This clause should detail how the property will be transferred or how the surviving co-owner will be compensated for the deceased's share of ownership.

Conclusion

Purchasing a property with a business partner can be a highly effective way to achieve homeownership or real estate investment goals without relying on traditional mortgage financing. However, it requires careful planning, clear communication, and a well-structured legal partnership agreement to ensure a smooth and mutually beneficial arrangement. By understanding the complexities of shared ownership, managing responsibilities effectively, and having a well-thought-out exit strategy, co-owners can protect their investment and maintain a positive, professional relationship throughout the duration of their partnership.

Chapter 17: The Art of Negotiation: Getting the Best Deal

Negotiation is a critical skill when it comes to buying a house without a traditional mortgage. Since you are exploring non-traditional financing options, understanding the art of negotiation can make all the difference in securing a great deal. Whether you are negotiating with a seller, private lender, or business partner, your ability to approach negotiations strategically will have a significant impact on the overall cost and structure of your home purchase. In this chapter, we will explore the key elements of negotiation, offer creative techniques to secure the best price, and guide you through overcoming common seller hesitations. We will also discuss how to use leverage and knowledge to your advantage, ensuring that you can approach the process with confidence and success.

Subsection 1: Negotiating Without a Traditional Mortgage

1.1 The Unique Nature of Creative Financing Negotiations

Traditional homebuyers rely on conventional mortgages through banks or lenders to finance their homes. However, when pursuing creative financing options, you will need to approach negotiations differently. Without a traditional mortgage, negotiations take place between you and the seller or a non-bank lender, meaning that the terms can be far more flexible.

The primary difference lies in the fact that the seller or lender may be more open to discussing non-standard terms. This could include:

- **Seller Financing**: The seller acts as the lender, allowing you to make payments directly to them instead of a bank.
- **Lease-to-Own**: Negotiating an option to rent the home with the right to purchase it later, often with a portion of rent payments going toward the purchase price.

- **Assumption of Existing Mortgage**: In some cases, you might negotiate to take over the seller's mortgage (if the lender allows), which could offer you a lower interest rate or more favorable terms.

When negotiating in these situations, you need to establish terms that are mutually beneficial, keeping in mind that the seller or lender may be taking on more risk by offering creative financing options.

1.2 Understand the Seller's Motivation

To negotiate effectively without a traditional mortgage, it is crucial to understand the seller's motivation. Are they eager to sell quickly? Are they looking for a higher price, or are they more focused on getting consistent payments? Sellers who are motivated to close a deal are more likely to entertain creative offers, such as owner financing or lower down payments.

For example, a seller who needs to sell quickly may be more open to offering seller financing if it guarantees a faster sale. On the other hand, a seller who is looking for a quick cash infusion may prefer a lease-to-own arrangement with an option for you to purchase the home within a specified period.

1.3 Building Rapport with the Seller

Negotiating without a mortgage is about building a relationship with the seller. The more they trust you and understand your reasons for choosing creative financing, the more willing they may be to negotiate favorable terms. Establish rapport early on in the process by being transparent and clear about your goals.

Consider the following tactics:

- **Transparency**: Be upfront about your financial situation and explain why a traditional mortgage is not ideal for you. This

can create a sense of understanding and make the seller more inclined to work with you.
- **Shared Vision**: Highlight how your purchase will benefit the seller. For example, if you are offering to buy their property using seller financing, you might emphasize how this arrangement allows them to receive steady payments over time while avoiding the hassle of traditional bank loans.

Subsection 2: Creative Techniques for Securing the Best Price

2.1 Exploring Flexible Terms

Creative financing often involves flexibility in terms of the agreement. Instead of focusing solely on price, consider negotiating other terms that benefit you. For example:

- **Flexible Down Payments**: If you lack the cash for a traditional down payment, propose a lower or staggered down payment over time.
- **Interest Rate Reductions**: Negotiate for a lower interest rate or a fixed interest rate to minimize long-term costs. Many sellers are willing to lower the interest rate if they see value in your proposal, especially if they can earn interest on the loan over time.
- **Rent-to-Own or Lease-to-Own Options**: Propose a rent-to-own arrangement in which part of your rent payment goes toward the purchase price of the property. This can be advantageous if you need time to save for a larger down payment or improve your credit score.

2.2 Bundling Financing with Other Services

In creative financing, you may also be able to bundle additional services or considerations to make your offer more appealing. This could include offering the seller assistance with moving costs, paying for minor repairs, or covering closing costs. These added benefits can sweeten the deal for the seller without significantly affecting the price of the home.

2.3 Look for Undervalued Properties

When negotiating with sellers, finding properties that are undervalued or distressed offers a unique opportunity for a better price. Sellers of such properties may be more motivated to offer creative financing options or accept a lower price, especially if they have been struggling to sell or if the property requires significant repairs.

2.4 Utilize a Third-Party Investor

If you do not have the full amount of capital required to purchase a property through creative financing, consider bringing in a third-party investor. This could be a business partner or an individual who is willing to contribute financially in exchange for a share of the profits, rental income, or property ownership.

Subsection 3: How to Overcome Seller Hesitations

3.1 Addressing the Seller's Concerns

One of the most significant challenges in creative financing negotiations is overcoming the seller's hesitations. Sellers may be wary of non-traditional financing options because they are unfamiliar or they fear financial risk. Addressing their concerns directly can help alleviate these worries and build trust.

Common concerns sellers may have include:

- **Risk of Non-Payment**: Sellers may worry that you will default on payments. Address this concern by offering a large

down payment or other security, such as collateral or a co-signer, to show that you are financially responsible.
- **Title or Ownership Transfer Issues**: With creative financing arrangements, the transfer of ownership may not be as straightforward as a traditional sale. Ensure that you explain how the title will be transferred and offer assurance that you will meet all legal and contractual obligations.

3.2 Offering Incentives for Seller Flexibility

Offering incentives can also ease a seller's hesitation. For example, you could propose that the seller continues to hold the property title until certain conditions are met (such as full payment or completion of repairs). This reduces the perceived risk for the seller while allowing you to secure the property.

3.3 Providing Legal and Financial Documentation

Sellers may be hesitant to engage in creative financing because they are unfamiliar with the process or unsure of its legality. Providing documentation from legal and financial professionals can reassure the seller that the transaction is legitimate and legally sound. This could include:

- **Seller Financing Agreement**: A legal document detailing the terms and conditions of the seller financing arrangement.
- **Escrow Account Setup**: If applicable, offer to set up an escrow account to ensure that payments are made on time and in the correct amounts.

Subsection 4: Using Leverage and Knowledge to Your Advantage

4.1 Conducting Market Research

When negotiating the best deal, leverage your knowledge of the market to your advantage. This includes researching comparable properties in the area, understanding market trends, and having a clear idea of the property's value. Knowledge of local property values, recent sales, and any potential for price increases or decreases will put you in a stronger position during negotiations.

4.2 Knowing the Seller's Timeline and Motivation

Understanding the seller's timeline is a powerful negotiating tool. If the seller is in a hurry to close, they may be more willing to negotiate on price or offer favorable terms. Conversely, if the seller is not under time pressure, you may have more room to negotiate a lower price or better financing terms.

4.3 Building a Competitive Edge

If you are competing with other buyers, use your knowledge of creative financing options to make your offer more appealing. Sellers who are familiar with traditional buyers may be drawn to the flexibility and quicker timelines that come with creative financing arrangements. Position yourself as a knowledgeable, capable buyer who can close quickly and with minimal hassle.

4.4 Negotiating with Confidence

Finally, confidence is key. When negotiating without a traditional mortgage, you need to be confident in your approach and in your understanding of the deal. Be prepared to make counter-offers and stand firm on the terms that are important to you, but always remain respectful and professional in your interactions.

Conclusion

120   How to Buy a House Without a Mortgage: Creative Financing Strategies

Mastering the art of negotiation is essential when purchasing a home without a traditional mortgage. By understanding the unique nature of creative financing, employing creative techniques, addressing seller concerns, and leveraging your knowledge, you can secure the best deal possible. Negotiation is not just about price; it's about creating a mutually beneficial agreement that works for both parties. With the right approach, you can navigate the world of creative financing with confidence and success.

How to Buy a House Without a Mortgage: Creative Financing Strategies

Chapter 18: Building a Network for Creative Financing

Building a network for creative financing is essential for anyone looking to purchase a home without relying on traditional mortgage methods. The world of creative financing often requires collaboration and support from a variety of professionals, as well as access to resources and investment opportunities that are not readily available through conventional channels. This chapter will delve into the importance of building a strong network, provide tips for assembling a team of experts, and highlight the best ways to find off-market deals, lenders, investors, and communities of like-minded individuals who share an interest in creative financing strategies. By the end of this chapter, you will understand the key players, resources, and strategies needed to create a successful network that supports your goal of purchasing a home creatively and without a mortgage.

Subsection 1: Building a Team of Professionals (Real Estate Agents, Lawyers, etc.)

1.1 The Role of Real Estate Agents in Creative Financing

A well-connected and knowledgeable real estate agent is an invaluable resource when purchasing a home without a traditional mortgage. Unlike conventional homebuyers, you will need an agent who understands creative financing options, such as seller financing, lease-to-own arrangements, or other non-traditional methods. The ideal agent should:

- Be experienced in negotiating terms beyond the traditional mortgage structure.
- Have access to properties that may not be listed on major real estate websites (off-market deals).
- Be able to guide you through the complexities of creative financing and legal implications.

When building your network, prioritize agents who specialize in investment properties or who have a history of working with buyers using alternative financing strategies. Such agents will have established relationships with sellers open to creative deals, which can be crucial when you're looking for opportunities outside the traditional market.

1.2 The Importance of Lawyers for Creative Financing

Legal expertise is essential in the world of creative financing. Since these types of transactions often involve unconventional agreements, such as seller financing or lease options, you need a lawyer who specializes in real estate law and can:

- Draft and review contracts to ensure that all terms are legally binding and protect your interests.
- Advise you on the tax implications of alternative financing arrangements.
- Ensure that any seller financing agreements are compliant with local laws and regulations.

Additionally, a lawyer can help with title searches, easements, or zoning laws, which are particularly important if you plan to make property improvements or alterations. For creative financing deals, a lawyer can also ensure the appropriate structuring of payments and ownership transfers, safeguarding both parties' rights.

1.3 The Role of Accountants and Financial Advisors

An accountant or financial advisor plays a vital role in assessing your financial situation and helping you structure creative financing deals that are sustainable in the long run. They can:

- Help you determine how much you can afford to invest upfront in a seller-financed deal or a rent-to-own arrangement.

123 How to Buy a House Without a Mortgage: Creative Financing Strategies

- Advise you on the most tax-efficient ways to structure payments or withdraw funds from retirement accounts if necessary.
- Assist with budgeting, understanding cash flow, and forecasting long-term financial impacts.

Given the unique nature of creative financing, consulting with professionals who can assess your finances from a broad perspective will ensure that your investments are viable and that you are protected from potential risks.

Subsection 2: Networking for Off-Market Property Deals

2.1 What are Off-Market Deals?

Off-market deals refer to properties that are not listed on traditional property search platforms or real estate marketplaces. These properties are often sold directly by the owner, and negotiations typically take place without the involvement of a real estate agent. Off-market deals are particularly attractive to those using creative financing because they often come with greater flexibility and room for negotiation.

2.2 Why Network for Off-Market Deals?

Networking for off-market deals allows you to access properties that are not publicly advertised, potentially giving you an edge over other buyers. Many sellers who choose not to list their property may be open to creative financing options, such as seller financing or lease-to-own arrangements. They may prefer to work directly with buyers and avoid paying commissions or fees to real estate agents.

Building a network of contacts that includes property owners, wholesalers, other investors, and even real estate agents who specialize in off-market deals can open up opportunities for creative financing. Additionally, these sellers are often more motivated to negotiate flexible terms if they are not tied to the constraints of a traditional sale.

2.3 How to Find Off-Market Deals

Networking for off-market deals involves proactive outreach and relationship-building. Here are some strategies:

- **Reach Out to Property Owners Directly**: You can send letters or postcards to owners of distressed or underdeveloped properties, offering to buy their homes using creative financing.
- **Join Real Estate Investment Groups**: Many real estate investors specialize in finding off-market deals. Attend meetups and conferences to network with these professionals who may have access to unlisted properties.
- **Work with Wholesalers**: Real estate wholesalers specialize in finding and securing off-market properties and selling them to investors at a markup. Establish relationships with wholesalers who may be able to connect you to sellers open to creative financing.
- **Leverage Social Media**: Join real estate investment groups and online forums where sellers or other investors might share opportunities for off-market properties. LinkedIn and Facebook groups can be excellent places to connect with sellers directly.
- **Use Public Records**: Research public records to find properties with liens, tax delinquencies, or pre-foreclosures. These properties may have motivated sellers who are open to creative financing solutions.

2.4 Building a Reputation in the Off-Market Space

When networking for off-market deals, it's essential to build a reputation as a serious buyer who can follow through with creative financing agreements. Being reliable, professional, and offering flexible terms will encourage sellers to consider your proposals. Reputation-building within your network of investors, real estate agents, and wholesalers will help ensure that you're notified of opportunities before they hit the open market.

Subsection 3: Finding the Right Lenders and Investors

3.1 Identifying Potential Lenders

Lenders are critical when exploring creative financing, particularly if you need additional capital or want to work with private lenders for non-traditional loans. Here's how to identify lenders who specialize in creative financing:

- **Private Lenders**: These are individuals or companies willing to lend money for real estate investments, typically at higher interest rates but with more flexible terms.
- **Hard Money Lenders**: These lenders provide short-term loans secured by the value of the property, which can be ideal if you're purchasing properties that need substantial repairs or renovations.
- **Crowdfunding Platforms**: Online real estate crowdfunding platforms connect investors with people looking for creative financing solutions. They can be a great resource for raising capital for a home purchase or for securing loans.

3.2 Building Relationships with Investors

Developing relationships with investors is essential for successful creative financing. Investors who specialize in real estate can offer guidance, mentorship, and financial backing, and they often have access to opportunities not available to the general public. Here's how to find the right investors:

- **Attend Networking Events**: Attend local real estate investment meetings, trade shows, and conferences to meet potential investors.
- **Use Online Platforms**: Platforms like BiggerPockets, LinkedIn, and real estate forums are great for connecting with other investors.
- **Leverage Your Existing Network**: If you know individuals who have experience with creative financing or real estate investment, ask for introductions to potential investors who may be interested in backing your projects.

Subsection 4: Joining Communities of Creative Financers

4.1 Why Join a Community of Creative Financers?

Being part of a community of creative financers provides you with a support system, access to new deals, and the opportunity to learn from experienced professionals. These communities offer the chance to share knowledge, learn about new financing strategies, and collaborate on joint ventures or partnerships.

4.2 Where to Find Creative Financing Communities

- **Real Estate Investment Associations (REIAs)**: These local or national organizations bring together real estate investors and professionals to share knowledge and opportunities.
- **Online Communities**: Platforms like BiggerPockets, Reddit's real estate investing subreddits, or Facebook groups are great places to join discussions and find resources on creative financing.
- **Mastermind Groups**: Many successful investors form mastermind groups where they meet regularly to discuss strategies, share opportunities, and collaborate on deals.

Joining a mastermind group can provide valuable mentorship and insight into creative financing.

4.3 Benefits of Joining Creative Financing Communities

- **Access to Knowledge**: Learn from other investors who have experience with creative financing strategies, such as seller financing, lease options, or subject-to deals.
- **Collaborative Opportunities**: By networking with other community members, you may find opportunities to partner on deals, pool resources, or jointly invest in real estate projects.
- **Mentorship and Support**: Having access to experienced mentors can significantly reduce the learning curve when navigating the world of creative financing. A supportive community can help you stay motivated and overcome challenges.

Conclusion

Building a network for creative financing is essential for anyone looking to purchase a property without a mortgage. By assembling a team of professionals, networking for off-market deals, finding the right lenders and investors, and joining communities of like-minded individuals, you can access opportunities, resources, and expertise that will help you achieve your goal of homeownership without traditional financing. Success in creative financing is not just about finding the right deals; it's about having a robust support system and leveraging the right connections to navigate the complexities of the real estate market.

How to Buy a House Without a Mortgage: Creative Financing Strategies

Chapter 19: Closing the Deal: What You Need to Know

Closing the deal is the final step in purchasing a home, whether you are using a traditional mortgage or employing a creative financing strategy. It's essential to fully understand what's involved in this process, especially when navigating alternative methods for acquiring a property. For those buying a home without a mortgage, closing can be more complex due to the unconventional nature of the financing arrangements, whether through seller financing, lease options, or other creative strategies. This chapter will provide a comprehensive guide on how to finalize a non-traditional home purchase, the required legal documents, how to protect yourself during the closing process, and the key steps to take after the deal is done.

Subsection 1: Steps to Finalize a Non-Traditional Home Purchase

1.1 Understand the Terms of the Deal

Before you can close a deal, it's essential to ensure that all terms and conditions of the non-traditional financing arrangement are clear and agreed upon. This may involve:

- **Reviewing the financing structure**: Is it a seller-financed deal? Are you entering into a rent-to-own arrangement or using a lease option? Make sure all parties understand the terms of payments, interest rates (if applicable), timelines, and contingencies.
- **Confirming payment terms**: Clarify how much of an upfront payment is required and whether monthly payments will be made, how they'll be structured, and the duration of the agreement.
- **Negotiating contingencies**: These can include clauses for inspection periods, financing requirements (for seller financing), or property condition repairs.

How to Buy a House Without a Mortgage: Creative Financing Strategies

1.2 Engage a Lawyer and Real Estate Agent (if applicable)

Although creative financing can often involve fewer intermediaries than a traditional home purchase, having a lawyer and real estate agent who specialize in non-traditional deals is important. These professionals will help ensure that:

- The agreement is legally sound.
- You understand the tax and legal implications of your financing structure.
- You are aware of any hidden clauses or potential risks within the contract.

1.3 Title Search and Property Inspection

A thorough title search is critical to ensure the property is free of legal encumbrances or disputes. You want to confirm that the seller has legal ownership and the authority to transfer the property. Likewise, completing a property inspection will help identify any underlying issues with the property that could affect your decision to move forward with the deal. Make sure the property is in a satisfactory condition before proceeding with the final steps of closing.

1.4 Finalizing the Financial Agreement

Once all terms are agreed upon, the financial agreement needs to be finalized. This can include:

- **Seller Financing Agreement**: If you are purchasing with seller financing, a promissory note is typically created that outlines the loan details, repayment schedule, and interest rates (if applicable).
- **Lease Option or Rent-to-Own Agreement**: These arrangements require a formal lease that includes the option to purchase the property within a specified time frame, often at a predetermined price.

1.5 Review Closing Costs

Even with non-traditional home buying methods, there may still be some closing costs associated with the transaction. These can include:

- **Title fees**: Title search and title insurance are essential in protecting both the buyer and seller from ownership disputes.
- **Recording fees**: These are necessary for the county or municipality to officially record the change of ownership.
- **Attorney and agent fees**: If you've engaged professionals to help with the process, their fees will need to be covered.

Subsection 2: Legal Documents and Paperwork Required

2.1 Seller Financing Agreement (Promissory Note)

In the case of seller financing, the most important document will be the **promissory note**, which acts as a legal contract between the buyer and the seller. This document outlines the:

- **Amount financed**: The total sum the buyer is borrowing from the seller.
- **Repayment schedule**: How often payments will be made (e.g., monthly, quarterly) and the payment amount.
- **Interest rate**: If applicable, the interest rate agreed upon.
- **Consequences of default**: What will happen if the buyer fails to make payments.
- **Loan term**: The duration over which the loan will be repaid.

2.2 Deed of Trust or Mortgage Agreement

Although not a traditional mortgage, a **deed of trust** or **mortgage agreement** may still be needed, especially in a seller-financed deal. This document secures the loan against the property, and it protects both the buyer and seller in case of default. It is typically filed with the local county office to make the financing official and part of the public record.

2.3 Purchase and Sale Agreement (PSA)

The **purchase and sale agreement** is the foundation of the entire transaction, setting out the terms and conditions of the sale. This document will include:

- The agreed-upon price.
- The terms of the sale, including any contingencies or clauses.
- A description of the property and the agreed-upon condition.
- Closing details, including the date and any responsibilities for closing costs.

2.4 Title Transfer Documents

At the closing, the **deed of sale** or **warranty deed** is executed. This legally transfers ownership of the property from the seller to the buyer. The deed should clearly reflect the buyer's name, the seller's name, and the legal description of the property.

2.5 Lease or Rent-to-Own Agreement

If the deal involves a lease-to-own or rent-to-own arrangement, this lease agreement should outline:

- The rent amount and payment due dates.
- The purchase option terms, including how the purchase price will be determined.
- Whether any portion of the rent will be credited toward the eventual purchase price.

2.6 Other Documents (Optional)

How to Buy a House Without a Mortgage: Creative Financing Strategies

Other documents may include power of attorney (if someone is signing on behalf of either party), insurance records, or an inspection report. Ensure all documents are reviewed and signed by both parties in the presence of witnesses, if required.

Subsection 3: How to Protect Yourself During Closing

3.1 Review Everything in Detail

Before signing any documents, ensure that every term, clause, and condition is clearly understood. Look out for:

- **Hidden clauses**: Some non-traditional agreements may contain clauses that benefit the seller but could be detrimental to you, such as escalated payments or large fees for early repayment.
- **Right of First Refusal**: In a rent-to-own agreement, this gives the seller the right to sell the property to someone else before you get the chance to exercise your purchase option.

3.2 Title Insurance and Escrow Accounts

Using **title insurance** ensures that you are protected against legal claims that could arise after the transaction. A title search ensures that the seller has a clear title to the property, and title insurance can protect you against unforeseen legal issues. Additionally, using an **escrow account** during closing is critical for ensuring that both parties meet their contractual obligations before the deal is finalized.

3.3 Working with a Lawyer

Even if you're using creative financing methods, it's crucial to have a lawyer present during closing to ensure everything is legally binding. They can:

How to Buy a House Without a Mortgage: Creative Financing Strategies

- Review the legal terms and conditions.
- Advise you on any last-minute changes.
- Ensure that your interests are protected, especially when dealing with non-standard agreements.

3.4 Secure Your Investment

Protect your investment by ensuring you understand the payment structure and your legal rights if the seller defaults (in the case of seller financing). Document everything and ensure all agreements are signed, witnessed, and filed accordingly.

Subsection 4: What to Do After the Deal is Done

4.1 Finalize Your Move-In or Transition

Once the deal is closed, you'll want to finalize your move-in or transition. If you've purchased the property outright (e.g., with seller financing), make sure to:

- **Update your address** with the post office, utility companies, and financial institutions.
- **Set up utilities**: Ensure that water, electricity, gas, and any other essential services are switched over to your name.

4.2 Managing Payments and Tracking Financial Obligations

If you've entered into a seller financing agreement or rent-to-own arrangement, it's important to:

- **Create a payment calendar** to stay on top of due dates.
- **Track your payment progress** and keep receipts or documentation to avoid disputes.

4.3 Maintain Property and Insurance

If you are managing a property through seller financing or another alternative method, make sure to:

- **Maintain the property**: Keep it in good condition to protect your investment.
- **Update insurance**: Ensure you have adequate home insurance to cover potential risks, including property damage or liability.

4.4 Explore Future Opportunities

Once you've successfully completed your first creative financing deal, start looking for more opportunities to grow your real estate portfolio. Keep networking, stay in touch with your financial advisors, and look for other sellers open to non-traditional financing options.

Conclusion

Closing a creative financing deal requires careful attention to detail, solid legal protections, and a clear understanding of the terms and conditions of your agreement. By following the proper steps—reviewing legal documents, ensuring financial security, and protecting your investment—you'll be well-prepared to close the deal successfully. With the right knowledge and preparation, closing a non-traditional home purchase can be a smooth and rewarding experience, bringing you closer to achieving homeownership without relying on a mortgage.

How to Buy a House Without a Mortgage: Creative Financing Strategies

Chapter 20: Moving into Your Debt-Free Home

Achieving debt-free homeownership is a major milestone. Whether you've used seller financing, a lease option, or another creative financing strategy, you've successfully navigated the complexities of acquiring a property without the burden of a traditional mortgage. Now, it's time to make the transition to life as a homeowner. This chapter will guide you through the essential steps of moving into your debt-free home, from the initial transition to budgeting for homeownership without a mortgage, long-term financial planning, and celebrating your success. By following these steps, you can ensure a smooth transition and build a secure financial future.

Subsection 1: How to Transition from Renting or Saving to Owning

1.1 The Psychological Shift from Tenant to Owner

One of the most significant changes when transitioning from renting to owning a home is the shift in mindset. As a renter, you likely had limited responsibility for repairs, maintenance, and other property-related issues. As an owner, you are now fully responsible for the condition of your home and its upkeep. This psychological transition involves:

- **Ownership Mentality**: Understanding that the home is now yours, and it is your responsibility to care for and maintain it.
- **Emotional Satisfaction**: Experiencing the pride of owning a home without the weight of a mortgage hanging over your head.
- **Empowerment**: You have the freedom to make decisions about renovations, interior design, and even how you live in your space.

1.2 Managing the Practical Transition

When you move from renting or saving to homeownership, there are some practical steps to consider:

- **Moving Process**: Hiring a professional moving company, or organizing a DIY move, can help ensure that the transition is as smooth as possible. Consider the time and energy needed to transport all your belongings to your new home.
- **Utility Setup**: Transfer utilities like electricity, water, gas, internet, and waste collection to your name. Make sure you understand any service setup fees, deposit requirements, and monthly costs.
- **Property Transfer and Inspection**: Once you've completed the sale or lease-to-own agreement, schedule any final inspections or assessments to ensure the property is in good condition and ready for you to move in.

1.3 Addressing New Responsibilities

As a homeowner, you take on new responsibilities, such as:

- **Maintenance and Repairs**: You are now responsible for taking care of the property, from fixing leaky faucets to maintaining the lawn and performing regular home inspections.
- **Insurance**: Homeowners' insurance is a must to protect your investment, covering potential risks like fire, theft, or natural disasters.
- **Property Taxes**: Be prepared for annual property taxes. Understanding how these taxes are assessed and ensuring that they are paid on time will prevent penalties.

Subsection 2: Budgeting for Homeownership Without a Mortgage

How to Buy a House Without a Mortgage: Creative Financing Strategies

2.1 Understanding the Financial Advantages of Debt-Free Ownership

One of the biggest benefits of owning your home without a mortgage is the elimination of monthly mortgage payments. However, there are still costs associated with homeownership. These include:

- **Property Taxes**: Depending on your location, property taxes can be substantial. It's important to budget for this annual expense and set aside the appropriate funds.
- **Insurance**: Homeowners' insurance, which covers damage to the property and liability, is essential. Additionally, consider supplemental insurance such as flood insurance, depending on your area.
- **Home Maintenance**: Regular maintenance, such as lawn care, HVAC servicing, plumbing, and roofing, will be part of your ongoing expenses. It's a good idea to set up a separate savings fund for home repairs and unexpected maintenance costs.
- **Utilities and Services**: Utility bills like electricity, water, and trash collection will now be your responsibility. If you're in a colder climate, heating and energy costs might be higher.

2.2 Building an Emergency Fund for Your Home

While you won't have a mortgage payment, it's still crucial to budget for the unforeseen costs of homeownership. A home emergency fund is essential to handle:

- **Unexpected Repairs**: Things like a broken water heater, leaky roof, or plumbing issues can crop up at any time. Having a financial buffer in place ensures that you're not caught off guard.
- **Long-Term Home Improvements**: You might want to renovate or upgrade parts of your home, such as installing a new kitchen, adding a bathroom, or landscaping the yard.

- **Disaster Preparedness**: In areas prone to natural disasters like hurricanes, floods, or wildfires, having a savings cushion for repairs or evacuation is critical.

2.3 Creating a Monthly Budget for Homeownership

With no monthly mortgage payment, you have more flexibility in your finances, but it's important to stay on top of other financial responsibilities. Creating a comprehensive budget will help you manage your homeownership costs effectively:

- **Track Monthly Expenses**: Keep a record of all the ongoing costs associated with your home (utilities, maintenance, taxes, insurance).
- **Set Aside Savings**: As part of your budgeting strategy, ensure that you're setting aside money for long-term savings and retirement, even with your new homeowner responsibilities.
- **Plan for Future Expenses**: Understand that the costs of owning a home can fluctuate from year to year, depending on things like property tax assessments and home improvements.

Subsection 3: Long-Term Financial Planning After a Non-Traditional Purchase

3.1 Asset Appreciation and Wealth Building

Owning a home without a mortgage allows you to build wealth over time through property appreciation. You can plan for the future by:

- **Tracking Property Value**: Regularly monitor the value of your property. Research market trends in your area and use this data to assess your home's appreciation.
- **Leveraging Your Equity**: Even without a traditional mortgage, your property's value can increase over time,

allowing you to tap into your equity for future investment opportunities or personal projects.

3.2 Retirement Planning

Without a mortgage, you may have more disposable income to put towards retirement savings. Consider:

- **Maximizing Retirement Accounts**: Take full advantage of tax-advantaged accounts like IRAs or 401(k)s, especially if you have the extra cash flow from no mortgage.
- **Diversification**: While homeownership is an asset, it's important to ensure your retirement savings are diversified into other investments, such as stocks, bonds, or mutual funds.

3.3 Estate Planning

Now that you own a home outright, it's essential to plan for the future. Create or update your will to ensure that your property is passed on according to your wishes. This will help avoid legal complications for your heirs and ensure that the home continues to benefit your family in the long term.

3.4 Preparing for Future Financial Goals

Think about how your homeownership will fit into your long-term financial goals. Whether you want to expand your real estate portfolio, start a new business, or save for future milestones, owning your debt-free home frees up resources to pursue these objectives.

Subsection 4: Celebrating Your Debt-Free Homeownership Journey

4.1 Reflecting on Your Accomplishment

Achieving debt-free homeownership is a monumental achievement. Celebrate your success by reflecting on:

- **Your Journey**: Consider the challenges you faced to get to this point. Whether it was finding creative financing options or navigating unconventional buying methods, acknowledge your determination and hard work.
- **Gratitude for Financial Freedom**: Enjoy the freedom that comes from not having a mortgage to pay each month. Take a moment to appreciate how far you've come and the financial independence that you've gained.

4.2 Hosting a Housewarming Celebration

What better way to mark the occasion than by hosting a housewarming party? Celebrate your new home and share the achievement with friends and family. This will not only give you a chance to show off your new space, but also connect with your loved ones and create lasting memories in your debt-free home.

4.3 Setting New Goals for Homeownership

While enjoying the moment, think about what's next. Perhaps you'd like to:

- **Renovate**: Start a home improvement project, whether that's remodeling a room or updating the landscaping.
- **Invest**: With the freedom of homeownership, you may decide to expand your investment strategy by purchasing additional properties or diversifying into other financial ventures.

4.4 Passing the Knowledge On

How to Buy a House Without a Mortgage: Creative Financing Strategies

Finally, celebrate by sharing your success story with others. Whether you write about your experience, mentor someone interested in debt-free homeownership, or simply share your insights with friends, you have the power to inspire others to follow in your footsteps.

Conclusion

Moving into your debt-free home is a life-changing experience. By transitioning thoughtfully from renting to owning, budgeting effectively, planning for the long term, and celebrating your journey, you can enjoy the many benefits of homeownership without the burden of mortgage debt. With careful financial planning and a focus on maintaining and appreciating your property, you can secure a prosperous future while living in your dream home.

Chapter 21: Building Financial Freedom Through Real Estate

Building financial freedom through real estate is one of the most powerful ways to create wealth over time. Real estate, when approached with creative financing strategies, offers the opportunity to generate income, appreciate in value, and provide the foundation for long-term financial security. In this chapter, we will explore how to use creative real estate financing to build wealth, leverage your home as an asset, and implement investment strategies that set you on the path to financial independence.

Subsection 1: Creating Long-Term Wealth Through Creative Real Estate Financing

1.1 Understanding the Power of Real Estate for Wealth Creation

Real estate is often regarded as one of the most stable and profitable forms of investment. By using creative financing strategies, such as seller financing, lease options, and rent-to-own agreements, you can acquire properties without relying on traditional bank loans or high-interest mortgages. This opens up the possibility of:

- **Cash Flow Generation**: By acquiring properties that generate rental income, you create a steady stream of passive income. This income can be used to reinvest in additional properties or cover living expenses, putting you on the path to financial freedom.
- **Appreciation**: Real estate tends to appreciate over time, especially in desirable locations. This appreciation allows you to build equity in your property, which can be leveraged for future investments or financial security.
- **Tax Benefits**: Real estate owners can take advantage of several tax benefits, including deductions for mortgage interest (when applicable), property taxes, depreciation, and repairs, which help increase overall returns on investment.

How to Buy a House Without a Mortgage: Creative Financing Strategies

1.2 The Role of Leverage in Building Wealth

Leverage is a powerful tool in real estate investing. In creative financing, leverage is used to acquire properties with minimal upfront capital, allowing you to control larger assets than you could afford outright. Some key leverage strategies include:

- **Seller Financing**: With seller financing, the seller acts as the lender, enabling you to bypass traditional banks and negotiate terms that work in your favour. This often results in lower interest rates and more flexible payment schedules.
- **Lease Options**: A lease option allows you to control a property and benefit from appreciation without initially owning it. This can be a great way to build equity over time, with the option to purchase the property later at a locked-in price.
- **Subject-To Financing**: This strategy involves taking control of a property and its mortgage without actually assuming the loan. You pay the seller's mortgage directly, while gaining control of the property.

1.3 Reinvesting for Long-Term Growth

Once you've acquired a property or multiple properties using creative financing methods, it's essential to reinvest the returns you generate for long-term growth. By doing so, you can scale your real estate portfolio and create a sustainable wealth-building strategy:

- **Compound Growth**: Reinvesting rental income into new property purchases allows for exponential growth. The more properties you acquire, the more your wealth will grow through rental income, appreciation, and equity buildup.
- **Diversification**: As you build your portfolio, diversify your investments by targeting different property types (residential, commercial, vacation rentals) or different geographical markets to reduce risk and increase potential returns.

Subsection 2: How to Leverage Your Home as an Asset

2.1 Understanding Home Equity

Home equity is the portion of your home's value that you actually own, calculated by subtracting the outstanding mortgage balance from the current market value of the home. Even if you own your home outright, the equity you have in the property can be used as a powerful tool to build wealth.

2.2 Using Home Equity for Investment Purposes

Your home can be leveraged to acquire additional assets. If you own your home free and clear, you can access this equity in several ways:

- **Home Equity Loan or Line of Credit (HELOC)**: By borrowing against your home's equity, you can access funds for investing in additional real estate, starting a business, or paying off high-interest debt. With a low-interest rate, this can be a very cost-effective way to finance further wealth-building endeavors.
- **Cash-Out Refinancing**: This allows you to refinance your property for more than you currently owe and take the difference in cash, which can be reinvested in other properties or used to cover living expenses.
- **Private Lending**: If you've built a strong relationship with other investors, you can use your property as collateral to offer private loans for other creative financing opportunities.

2.3 Renting Your Home for Cash Flow

If your property is in a desirable location, you can rent it out for cash flow. By becoming a landlord, you can generate passive income while your property continues to appreciate. Renting out part of your

How to Buy a House Without a Mortgage: Creative Financing Strategies

home, or even converting it into a multi-unit rental, allows you to use the property to create income and build wealth over time.

Subsection 3: Real Estate Investment Strategies for Future Growth

3.1 Buy and Hold Strategy

One of the most common and effective strategies in real estate is the "buy and hold" strategy, which involves purchasing properties and holding them for long-term appreciation and rental income. By using creative financing methods to acquire properties with little or no down payment, you can begin earning rental income immediately, while benefiting from the property's appreciation over time.

- **Advantages**: Long-term growth, stable income, and equity building. This strategy works well in markets with rising property values.
- **Challenges**: The strategy requires long-term commitment and may involve property management responsibilities.

3.2 Fix and Flip

Another popular strategy is the fix-and-flip method, which involves buying a property that needs repairs, making necessary improvements, and then selling it for a profit. This strategy is ideal for those with renovation skills or access to contractors.

- **Advantages**: Potential for quick profits if done correctly, especially in a hot market.
- **Challenges**: Fixing and flipping properties can be costly, and there's a higher level of risk, especially in volatile markets. Using creative financing methods, like seller financing or lease options, can reduce your initial investment and maximize profit margins.

3.3 Vacation Rentals and Short-Term Rentals

With platforms like Airbnb and Vrbo, short-term rentals have become an increasingly profitable investment strategy. By purchasing properties in high-demand tourist areas or cities with strong rental demand, you can generate higher rental income compared to long-term rentals.

- **Advantages**: Potential for high rental yields, especially in tourist hotspots.
- **Challenges**: Increased maintenance, more management involvement, and fluctuating rental demand.

3.4 Real Estate Investment Trusts (REITs)

For those who want exposure to real estate without the hassle of property management, Real Estate Investment Trusts (REITs) can be a great option. REITs are companies that own or finance income-producing real estate and allow investors to buy shares, similar to investing in stocks.

- **Advantages**: Diversification, passive income, and the ability to invest with smaller amounts of capital.
- **Challenges**: Lower control over specific properties and possible volatility in the market.

3.5 Wholesaling

Wholesaling in real estate involves finding properties at a discounted price and then selling the contract to another investor for a profit. This strategy requires little to no capital upfront and works well if you have good networking and negotiation skills.

- **Advantages**: Low financial risk and quick turnaround.
- **Challenges**: It can be difficult to find profitable deals consistently, and it requires strong negotiation skills and market knowledge.

Subsection 4: Continuing the Journey Toward Financial Independence

4.1 Creating a Sustainable Income Stream

Building financial freedom through real estate is not just about acquiring property—it's about creating a sustainable income stream that generates wealth without the need for active, day-to-day involvement. By focusing on cash-flowing properties, such as rental homes or commercial properties, you can create a passive income stream that continues to provide for your financial needs.

4.2 Financial Independence Through Real Estate Investment

The ultimate goal of using real estate to achieve financial freedom is to create enough passive income that you no longer need to work for money. With multiple income-generating properties, you can achieve a state of financial independence, where your investments sustain your lifestyle.

- **Action Steps**: Continue acquiring properties, reinvest your earnings, diversify your portfolio, and focus on long-term wealth building through cash flow and appreciation.

4.3 Scaling Your Real Estate Portfolio

Once you've established a foundation of rental properties or other real estate investments, consider scaling your portfolio by adding more properties. The key to scaling is maintaining a balance between managing risk and maximizing returns. Use creative financing techniques to acquire properties without putting too much capital at risk.

4.4 Financial Freedom Mindset

To truly achieve financial independence through real estate, it's important to maintain a mindset that focuses on long-term wealth-building and financial freedom. This means:

- Avoiding lifestyle inflation and continuing to reinvest your profits.
- Focusing on building sustainable, scalable assets.
- Being patient and consistent in your efforts.

Conclusion

Building financial freedom through real estate is not a get-rich-quick scheme, but a deliberate, long-term strategy. By employing creative financing methods, leveraging your home as an asset, and implementing smart investment strategies, you can create lasting wealth and achieve financial independence. The journey requires knowledge, discipline, and patience, but the rewards are worth the effort. Whether you're a first-time investor or a seasoned pro, real estate offers an unparalleled opportunity to build wealth and secure your financial future.

How to Buy a House Without a Mortgage: Creative Financing Strategies

Chapter 22: Overcoming Common Obstacles

Purchasing a home without a mortgage using creative financing strategies can be a highly rewarding journey, but it comes with its set of challenges. Whether you're facing misconceptions about debt-free homeownership, navigating rejections in the creative financing process, or dealing with market fluctuations and risks, understanding how to overcome these obstacles will empower you to move forward with confidence. In this chapter, we will address the most common obstacles that buyers face when pursuing a debt-free home purchase and provide practical solutions to tackle each challenge effectively.

Subsection 1: Addressing Common Fears and Misconceptions About Debt-Free Homeownership

1.1 Fear of the Unknown and Misunderstanding of Debt-Free Ownership

One of the most common obstacles people face when pursuing debt-free homeownership is the fear of the unknown. The traditional homebuying process, which typically involves securing a mortgage, is deeply ingrained in our culture. When people consider alternative financing options, they may be hesitant or unsure of how to navigate these less conventional paths. Common misconceptions include:

- **Belief that debt-free homeownership is impossible**: Many people mistakenly think that buying a home without a mortgage is simply not feasible. However, through creative financing strategies like seller financing, lease options, and subject-to deals, it is possible to purchase a home without relying on a traditional mortgage.
- **Fear of being scammed or taken advantage of**: The unfamiliarity with creative financing methods can also create fear of fraud or exploitation. Buyers might worry that they'll

be stuck in unfavorable deals or face hidden costs. However, with proper due diligence and legal safeguards, these risks can be minimized.
- **Skepticism about financial stability**: Some individuals are concerned that going debt-free in homeownership might limit their ability to access future credit or loan options. However, focusing on building wealth through real estate and creative financing can actually offer more financial freedom in the long term, without the burden of a large debt.

1.2 Overcoming Fear Through Education and Preparation

The key to overcoming these fears and misconceptions lies in education and preparation:

- **Do Your Research**: Understand the different types of creative financing methods and how they work. Learn about seller financing, lease options, and other strategies that allow for a debt-free purchase.
- **Work with Trusted Professionals**: Hire real estate agents, lawyers, or consultants who specialize in creative financing. They can guide you through the process, answer questions, and ensure that you're making informed decisions.
- **Consult with Experienced Buyers**: Talk to others who have successfully purchased homes through alternative financing. Their experience can provide insights and reassure you that it is possible to buy a home without a mortgage.

Subsection 2: How to Handle Rejections or Challenges in the Creative Financing Process

How to Buy a House Without a Mortgage: Creative Financing Strategies

2.1 Rejections from Sellers or Lenders

Another common obstacle in the creative financing process is encountering rejections. Sellers may not be familiar with creative financing methods or may not be open to them. Similarly, investors or lenders might be unwilling to provide alternative financing options. Here's how you can handle these challenges:

- **Seller Hesitation**: If a seller is hesitant to enter into a creative financing agreement, it's important to understand their concerns and address them directly. Be transparent about how seller financing works and emphasize the benefits they would receive, such as a steady stream of income and the potential for a quicker sale.
- **Lender Refusal**: If you face rejection from a lender or private investor, don't be discouraged. Rejections are a natural part of the process. Consider exploring other financing methods or building a stronger network of investors. You can also look for non-traditional lenders who specialize in creative financing.
- **Challenge of Finding Suitable Sellers or Properties**: Finding properties that fit your specific creative financing criteria can take time. But perseverance is key. Utilize networking, attend real estate events, and use online platforms to discover off-market deals that are better suited to your strategy.

2.2 Strategies for Overcoming Rejection

- **Build Strong Relationships**: Approach sellers, lenders, and investors with empathy and a willingness to understand their needs. Building strong relationships based on trust will increase your chances of success.
- **Adapt Your Offer**: If a seller or lender turns down your initial offer, consider adjusting your terms. Flexibility can be

key to overcoming rejections. Propose a deal that better fits their goals while still serving your needs.
- **Persevere**: Rejections may be discouraging, but they are part of the process. Keep refining your approach and learning from each experience. Eventually, you will find the right sellers or investors who are open to creative financing.

Subsection 3: Dealing with Market Fluctuations and Risk Management

3.1 Understanding Market Fluctuations

Market fluctuations and economic conditions play a significant role in the success of any real estate transaction. Creative financing strategies rely heavily on market dynamics such as interest rates, property values, and rental demand. When market conditions change, it can affect your ability to close deals or maintain profitability. Key challenges include:

- **Price Volatility**: Property values can fluctuate, making it difficult to assess the true value of a property. If you've agreed to purchase a property using creative financing, a drop in market value can put you at risk of overpaying or having negative equity.
- **Interest Rate Changes**: While creative financing deals often avoid traditional mortgages, some methods (like seller financing) may still involve interest rates that are influenced by market conditions. A sudden increase in interest rates can impact the affordability of your deal.
- **Liquidity Issues**: In a fluctuating market, it may become more difficult to sell or rent properties. This can create cash flow problems if you depend on rental income to cover property expenses.

How to Buy a House Without a Mortgage: Creative Financing Strategies

3.2 Risk Management Strategies

To protect yourself from market fluctuations and ensure long-term success in creative real estate financing, use the following strategies:

- **Due Diligence**: Always conduct thorough research before entering any creative financing agreement. This includes researching the local market, analyzing property values, and understanding rental demand in the area.
- **Diversification**: Don't put all your eggs in one basket. Consider diversifying your real estate investments to mitigate the risk of market downturns. Having properties in different locations or property types can reduce exposure to local market volatility.
- **Maintain an Emergency Fund**: Keep a financial cushion to cover unexpected expenses or periods of low cash flow. This will give you peace of mind and help you weather market fluctuations.

3.3 Adaptive Strategies for Changing Markets

- **Reevaluate Your Property Choices**: In times of market uncertainty, consider shifting your focus toward more resilient types of real estate, such as rental properties in high-demand areas or properties that generate short-term rental income.
- **Adjust Financing Terms**: If interest rates rise or property values drop, be prepared to renegotiate the terms of your creative financing deal. Flexibility will help you navigate changing market conditions.

Subsection 4: How to Adapt Your Strategy for Success

4.1 The Importance of Flexibility and Adaptability

One of the key components of successful creative financing is the ability to adapt your strategy to the circumstances at hand. Real estate markets, personal finances, and investment opportunities all change over time. If you want to succeed in buying a home without a mortgage, you must be willing to adjust your approach as needed. Some ways to adapt include:

- **Exploring New Financing Methods**: If your initial approach doesn't yield results, consider exploring different creative financing strategies. Options like lease options, seller financing, or subject-to deals may offer better solutions as circumstances change.
- **Adjusting Your Goals**: Your financial goals may evolve over time. Be open to adjusting your homeownership or investment goals to reflect changes in your life, career, or market conditions.

4.2 Building Resilience in Your Approach

Successful creative financiers understand that the journey is full of ups and downs. Developing resilience means:

- **Learning from Setbacks**: Every challenge is an opportunity to learn. If one deal falls through or a market downturn occurs, take the time to assess what went wrong and apply those lessons to future opportunities.
- **Staying Focused on Long-Term Goals**: While short-term challenges may arise, always keep your long-term financial goals in mind. Consistent effort and a long-term perspective are essential for success in real estate.

4.3 Continuous Education and Networking

Adapting your strategy also involves staying informed about changes in the market, new financing methods, and emerging trends. Regularly attend industry events, read relevant books and articles, and network with other investors and professionals to stay ahead of the curve.

Conclusion

Overcoming obstacles in the creative financing process requires a combination of knowledge, adaptability, and persistence. By addressing common fears, handling rejections with grace, managing market fluctuations, and continuously adapting your strategy, you can achieve success in buying a home without a mortgage. The ability to navigate challenges and persist through setbacks is a hallmark of successful real estate investors. With the right mindset and approach, you can turn creative financing into a powerful tool for achieving your dream of debt-free homeownership.

Chapter 23: How to Protect Your Home and Investments

Buying a home without a traditional mortgage using creative financing strategies is a powerful way to secure financial freedom. However, as with any significant investment, it's essential to take steps to protect both your home and your financial assets. This chapter will guide you through strategies that safeguard your property, including insurance, legal protections, contract structures, long-term maintenance, and estate planning. By implementing these protective measures, you can ensure that your home remains a secure and valuable asset for years to come.

Subsection 1: Property Insurance and Legal Protection for Non-Traditional Home Buyers

1.1 Understanding Property Insurance for Debt-Free Homeownership

Property insurance is one of the most important forms of protection for homeowners, regardless of how they finance their property. It covers you in the event of damage to your home due to unforeseen circumstances such as fire, theft, or natural disasters. However, when purchasing a home using creative financing methods, there are unique considerations that you need to account for:

- **Title Insurance**: This is crucial when you are purchasing a home using non-traditional financing methods like seller financing or lease options. Title insurance protects you from any legal disputes over property ownership that may arise after closing. For example, there may be an undiscovered lien or claim on the property. With title insurance, you are safeguarded from these potential issues.
- **Homeowner's Insurance**: In addition to the mandatory title insurance, homeowner's insurance will protect your property

How to Buy a House Without a Mortgage: Creative Financing Strategies

against a wide range of risks, including fire, theft, vandalism, and certain natural disasters. It's important to choose a policy that adequately covers the full value of the property.
- **Liability Insurance**: This type of insurance protects you if someone is injured on your property. If you plan on renting out part of your home or using it for business purposes (e.g., renting a room through Airbnb), liability insurance is crucial.

1.2 Legal Protections for Non-Traditional Home Buyers

Beyond property insurance, legal protection plays a crucial role in ensuring that your investments remain secure. This is particularly relevant for creative financing strategies, where you may be dealing with unconventional contract structures and riskier investments. Key areas of legal protection include:

- **Legal Due Diligence**: Before committing to any creative financing deal, work with a real estate lawyer who can help you navigate the legal complexities. They will ensure that the property title is clear and that all contracts are legally binding and enforceable. This is especially important for seller financing or lease-to-own arrangements, where standard home-buying procedures may not apply.
- **Secure Contracts and Agreements**: Your contract should be crafted with legal protections in mind. This includes clear terms and contingencies, such as payment schedules, dispute resolution processes, and steps to follow in the event of non-compliance. Having a lawyer draft or review these documents will provide you with additional security.
- **Risk of Fraud**: Creative financing often involves private lenders or individuals, which can sometimes lead to fraudulent situations. Protect yourself by ensuring that all agreements are formalized in writing, with terms and conditions clearly outlined. You should also work with reputable individuals, especially when using non-traditional lenders or engaging in seller financing.

Subsection 2: Structuring Contracts to Avoid Disputes

2.1 Importance of Clear and Detailed Contracts

One of the most effective ways to protect your home and investments is to structure your contracts in a way that minimizes the potential for disputes. This involves creating a clear and comprehensive agreement that outlines all aspects of the transaction. Key elements to consider include:

- **Payment Terms**: Be specific about the payment amount, frequency, and method. Include a clear schedule with due dates and penalties for late payments. For example, if you're using seller financing, ensure that the terms clearly define the principal amount, interest rate, and repayment period.
- **Contingencies**: Include contingencies in the contract that allow for flexibility in case unforeseen circumstances arise. For example, if the home suffers significant damage due to a natural disaster, a contingency clause can allow for delayed payments or the option to cancel the agreement.
- **Default Clauses**: Define what will happen in the event of a default. Whether it's a missed payment or violation of terms, having a clear default clause will protect you by ensuring that there's a predefined process for addressing breaches of contract.
- **Dispute Resolution**: Set clear guidelines for how disputes will be handled. This might include mediation or arbitration as an alternative to costly litigation. A well-structured dispute resolution clause ensures that both parties have a clear understanding of how conflicts will be resolved, reducing the risk of costly legal battles.
- **Title and Ownership Clauses**: When purchasing through non-traditional methods, make sure that the title to the

property is transferred properly and that you hold the full ownership rights as per the contract.

2.2 Working with Legal Professionals

While structuring your contracts, it's highly recommended that you involve a real estate lawyer. Their expertise can help you:

- Ensure all legal language is properly worded.
- Identify potential loopholes or areas of risk.
- Ensure compliance with state and local laws.
- Provide you with legal recourse options in the event of a dispute.

Subsection 3: Long-Term Maintenance and Financial Care for Your Property

3.1 Importance of Regular Maintenance

Maintaining your property is key to protecting your long-term investment. A well-maintained home retains its value and ensures that you avoid costly repairs down the line. Below are key considerations for maintaining a property:

- **Routine Inspections**: Regularly inspect the condition of the property. Check for issues like leaks, cracks, and signs of water damage. Catching small problems early can prevent them from turning into major, expensive repairs.
- **Upgrades and Improvements**: Regular home improvements, such as updating the kitchen or replacing old roofing, will ensure that your property remains in good condition. These upgrades can also increase the resale value of your property, offering a strong return on investment.

- **Landscaping and Exterior Maintenance**: Maintaining the exterior of the home is just as important as interior upkeep. This includes taking care of the garden, lawn, and even the paintwork of the property. Curb appeal matters for long-term investment protection.
- **Energy Efficiency**: Implementing energy-efficient upgrades, such as installing energy-efficient windows or appliances, will reduce your utility bills and make your property more attractive to future buyers or tenants.

3.2 Financial Care for Your Property

In addition to physical maintenance, it's important to care for your property's finances:

- **Set Aside Funds for Repairs**: Always allocate a portion of your income for property repairs and upgrades. A typical recommendation is to set aside about 1% of the property value annually for repairs and maintenance.
- **Property Taxes and Insurance Premiums**: Keep track of property taxes and insurance premiums. Failure to pay property taxes can result in liens or foreclosure, while inadequate insurance could leave you financially vulnerable in the event of damage or theft.

Subsection 4: Estate Planning and Protecting Your Debt-Free Asset

4.1 The Importance of Estate Planning

Estate planning is critical for ensuring that your debt-free home and other investments are passed on according to your wishes. Estate planning involves creating a legal framework that dictates how your assets will be handled after your passing. Without proper estate

How to Buy a House Without a Mortgage: Creative Financing Strategies

planning, your assets could end up in probate or be distributed in a way that is not in line with your intentions.

- **Wills and Trusts**: One of the primary components of estate planning is creating a will or trust that specifies how your property should be transferred. A trust allows for more control over how your property is distributed, potentially avoiding probate and offering tax benefits.
- **Power of Attorney**: Assign a power of attorney to someone you trust who can make financial or legal decisions for you in the event you become incapacitated.
- **Health Care Directives**: In addition to protecting your physical assets, it's important to ensure that you have health care directives in place, specifying your preferences for medical treatment if you are unable to make decisions for yourself.

4.2 Protecting Your Asset from Creditors

Even though you own your home debt-free, there are circumstances where creditors may attempt to lay claim to it. These include personal lawsuits, business debt, or divorce proceedings. Some strategies for protecting your home include:

- **Homestead Exemptions**: Many states offer homestead exemptions that protect your primary residence from certain types of creditors. Check your local laws to understand how you can protect your home.
- **Asset Protection Trusts**: For those with substantial assets, setting up an asset protection trust can help shield your home and other properties from legal claims.

Conclusion

Protecting your home and investments involves a comprehensive approach that includes property insurance, legal protections, structuring clear contracts, ongoing maintenance, and estate planning. By safeguarding your home through these strategies, you ensure not only the long-term preservation of your property's value but also the financial security of your debt-free lifestyle. Through diligence and foresight, you can protect your investment and enjoy the rewards of homeownership without the burden of traditional mortgage debt.

How to Buy a House Without a Mortgage: Creative Financing Strategies

Chapter 24: Future Trends in Creative Financing

The real estate landscape is constantly evolving, and creative financing methods are becoming more popular as individuals and investors seek alternatives to traditional mortgage options. This chapter explores the future of homeownership without mortgages, emerging trends in real estate financing, the role of technology in transforming creative financing, and what to expect in the next decade for buyers and investors looking to use creative methods to secure property. As these trends shape the market, it's important to stay informed about how they will affect the way homes are bought, sold, and financed in the future.

Subsection 1: The Future of Homeownership Without Mortgages

1.1 The Changing Landscape of Homeownership

As more buyers seek debt-free living, the traditional concept of homeownership through a conventional mortgage is becoming less of a necessity. Homeownership without a mortgage is being embraced as a path to financial freedom, allowing individuals to avoid long-term debt and interest payments. Over the next decade, there will be a shift in the way people approach homeownership, driven by several key factors:

- **Rise in Seller Financing**: As the market shifts, we are likely to see an increase in seller financing deals. With more individuals becoming aware of the option to finance homes directly through the seller, this trend will continue to grow. This provides more flexibility and fewer barriers to homeownership, especially for first-time buyers who might not meet the qualifications for a traditional mortgage.

- **Lease-to-Own Options**: Lease-to-own agreements are gaining popularity because they provide a way for tenants to build equity over time. Buyers can gradually move toward homeownership, and sellers get consistent rental income. This structure is expected to grow as both parties seek more flexible, less-risky financial arrangements.
- **Cooperative Housing Models**: Cooperative housing, where residents collectively own and manage a property, is gaining traction as a way to purchase homes without a traditional mortgage. These models can lower the financial barrier to entry by pooling resources and sharing ownership responsibilities.

1.2 The Shift Toward Debt-Free Living

More consumers are rejecting traditional mortgage structures and opting for creative financing methods that allow them to own a home without taking on substantial debt. This shift is being fueled by:

- **Rising Interest Rates**: As interest rates increase, traditional mortgage payments can become unaffordable. This prompts potential buyers to explore creative financing options like seller financing, rent-to-own agreements, and crowd-funded real estate deals, which typically have fewer fees and lower costs.
- **Growing Awareness of Financial Freedom**: As people seek greater financial independence, buying a house without a mortgage offers a way to remove the financial burden of debt. The desire to live mortgage-free is becoming more common, and as this trend grows, the options available for debt-free homeownership will expand.

Subsection 2: Emerging Trends in Real Estate Financing

How to Buy a House Without a Mortgage: Creative Financing Strategies

2.1 Crowdfunding and Peer-to-Peer Lending

One of the most exciting developments in the world of creative financing is the rise of crowdfunding and peer-to-peer (P2P) lending platforms. These platforms allow individuals to pool resources to fund home purchases and real estate investments.

- **Real Estate Crowdfunding**: Platforms like Fundrise and RealtyMogul are changing the way investors fund properties. These platforms allow individuals to invest small amounts into larger real estate projects, which could be used for home purchases or larger developments. Homebuyers can also potentially leverage these platforms to raise funds for non-traditional purchases or investments in properties.
- **P2P Lending**: Peer-to-peer lending platforms like Prosper and LendingClub provide an alternative to traditional bank loans, allowing individuals to obtain funds directly from other people, typically at lower interest rates. As these platforms become more common, more people will turn to them as a viable source of financing for home purchases.

2.2 Seller Financing and Rent-to-Own Agreements

- **Seller Financing Growth**: As traditional mortgage lenders tighten their requirements, seller financing becomes an increasingly attractive alternative. In seller financing arrangements, the buyer makes payments directly to the seller instead of a bank or financial institution. This can bypass many of the stringent requirements of traditional mortgage lenders, making homeownership accessible to more people.
- **Rent-to-Own Models**: Rent-to-own agreements are also gaining momentum, especially among first-time buyers who want to "test out" homeownership before fully committing. These agreements allow buyers to rent the property with the option to buy it later, often with a portion of the rent contributing toward the purchase price.

Subsection 3: How Technology Is Changing the Creative Financing Landscape

3.1 The Role of Blockchain in Real Estate Transactions

Blockchain technology is beginning to make waves in real estate financing by simplifying and securing transactions. Blockchain can reduce fraud, speed up the closing process, and make transactions more transparent. Here's how:

- **Tokenization of Real Estate**: Blockchain technology allows for the tokenization of real estate assets, meaning real estate can be broken down into small, tradable units that can be sold to investors or used as collateral for financing. This creates opportunities for fractional ownership, where multiple investors can own portions of a single property.
- **Smart Contracts**: Blockchain enables the use of smart contracts, which automatically execute terms once conditions are met. These contracts could be used for creative financing strategies, like seller financing or rent-to-own agreements, reducing the need for intermediaries and minimizing the potential for disputes.

3.2 Digital Platforms and Real Estate Marketplaces

Digital platforms and marketplaces are revolutionizing how buyers and sellers find and finance homes. These platforms help make creative financing strategies more accessible by connecting buyers with sellers, lenders, and investors.

- **Online Marketplaces for Seller Financing**: Websites like OwnerFinancedHomes.com allow buyers and sellers to find each other and negotiate financing terms directly. This

eliminates the need for traditional financial intermediaries and can make homeownership more affordable and accessible.
- **Peer-to-Peer Platforms for Alternative Financing**: These platforms are growing in popularity and serve as a marketplace for non-traditional financing options, such as crowdfunded real estate investments, seller financing, and other creative financing methods.

3.3 AI and Machine Learning in Real Estate

Artificial Intelligence (AI) and machine learning are starting to be used in real estate to better predict property values, identify investment opportunities, and optimize financing strategies. AI can help real estate buyers and investors make smarter decisions by:

- **Predicting Market Trends**: AI can analyze vast amounts of data to predict the best times to buy, sell, or invest in real estate, allowing for more informed decision-making in creative financing strategies.
- **Assessing Risk and Creditworthiness**: AI can help lenders or sellers assess the creditworthiness of potential buyers without relying on traditional credit scores. This opens the door for more people to access alternative financing options, especially those with unconventional financial backgrounds.

Subsection 4: What to Expect in the Next Decade

4.1 Increased Accessibility to Creative Financing Options

The next decade will see a continued expansion of non-traditional financing options for real estate buyers. As more individuals and companies realize the benefits of alternative financing, it's expected that:

- **Seller Financing Will Become More Common**: As interest rates rise and banks become more stringent in their lending criteria, many homeowners and investors will turn to seller financing as a flexible option. This allows them to create deals with terms that suit both parties while providing homebuyers with an opportunity to bypass the traditional mortgage system.
- **Alternative Lenders Will Continue to Grow**: Peer-to-peer lending, crowdfunding, and other non-bank lenders will continue to rise. These platforms will evolve to offer more options, enabling people to access funds for home purchases, renovations, and investments with greater ease and flexibility.

4.2 A Greater Shift Toward Financial Independence and Ownership

- **Debt-Free Living as a Trend**: The desire for financial freedom and debt-free living will become increasingly popular in the coming years. More people will seek homeownership options that allow them to own property without relying on a traditional mortgage. This will lead to a greater adoption of rent-to-own, seller financing, and cooperative housing models.
- **The Demise of Traditional Mortgages**: While traditional mortgage systems will still exist, their role in homeownership will gradually decrease as alternative financing methods grow. Buyers will have more options to bypass mortgage lenders and avoid long-term debt, contributing to a financial independence movement.

Conclusion

The future of creative financing is bright, with numerous opportunities for homebuyers and investors to take control of their

How to Buy a House Without a Mortgage: Creative Financing Strategies

financial future. With new technologies, evolving real estate strategies, and a growing desire for debt-free living, creative financing options will become more mainstream. The trends discussed in this chapter—crowdfunding, blockchain, peer-to-peer lending, and evolving property models—will transform the way we approach real estate transactions. As these trends continue to evolve, it's clear that the next decade will bring exciting changes to the creative financing landscape, making it easier than ever to buy a house without a traditional mortgage. By staying ahead of these trends and embracing innovative financing methods, you can secure your financial future and become part of the growing movement toward alternative homeownership.

How to Buy a House Without a Mortgage: Creative Financing Strategies

Conclusion: Unlocking a Debt-Free Future

Buying a home without a traditional mortgage is a powerful step toward financial freedom, independence, and long-term wealth. This conclusion reflects on the journey you've undertaken to achieve homeownership without a mortgage and provides essential insights and strategies for maintaining success in real estate and beyond. Whether you've just completed your purchase or are still considering how to proceed with creative financing, the journey toward a debt-free future is full of opportunities.

In this section, we will reflect on your journey to homeownership, explore the numerous benefits of living without a mortgage, offer final tips for continued success in real estate and financial freedom, and outline the necessary next steps to take in order to realize your dream home. Embrace these strategies and principles to unlock the doors to a truly debt-free future.

Subsection 1: Reflecting on Your Journey to Homeownership

1.1 Acknowledging the Achievement of Debt-Free Homeownership

Reflecting on the journey of purchasing a home without a mortgage is crucial. It requires acknowledging the hard work, research, and strategic decisions you've made to get to this point. Buying a home through creative financing methods—whether through seller financing, lease-to-own, or other alternatives—is a significant achievement, often requiring dedication, perseverance, and out-of-the-box thinking.

Your journey may have involved:

- **Overcoming fears** related to non-traditional financing.

How to Buy a House Without a Mortgage: Creative Financing Strategies

- **Educating yourself** on creative financing strategies and their potential benefits.
- **Building a network** of professionals who supported you, including real estate agents, investors, and lenders.
- **Negotiating complex deals** that aligned with your financial goals.

This journey is not just about purchasing a property—it's a milestone in your broader quest for financial independence. Reflecting on this can help you stay focused on your future goals and empower you to tackle further challenges with confidence.

1.2 Celebrating the Milestones

As you move forward, take time to celebrate key milestones along the way. Whether it's the first time you signed a creative financing agreement or the moment you officially moved into your home, each victory brings you closer to your goal of financial freedom.

Take a moment to appreciate:

- **The financial discipline** it took to navigate creative financing options.
- **The empowerment** of making choices that align with your values and long-term goals.
- **The sense of accomplishment** in securing a property without taking on crippling debt.

Recognizing these moments will help you build confidence and momentum as you continue to build wealth.

Subsection 2: The Benefits of Living Without a Mortgage

How to Buy a House Without a Mortgage: Creative Financing Strategies

2.1 Financial Freedom and Reduced Financial Burden

Living without a mortgage frees up substantial resources that would otherwise be tied up in monthly payments, interest rates, and long-term debt. This newfound financial flexibility can be used for numerous opportunities, including:

- **Investing in further property acquisitions**: Without the burden of a mortgage, you can save or invest in real estate more efficiently, building a portfolio of debt-free properties.
- **Expanding savings and retirement funds**: With more disposable income, you can allocate more toward retirement savings, investment accounts, and emergency funds.
- **Personal freedom**: Without worrying about hefty mortgage payments, you can focus on personal goals, such as travel, education, or pursuing passions that enrich your life.

2.2 Psychological Benefits of Homeownership Without Debt

Besides the obvious financial advantages, living without a mortgage provides a sense of psychological relief:

- **Reduced stress**: The constant worry of monthly mortgage payments and long-term debt is lifted, allowing you to enjoy your home and your life without the weight of financial obligations.
- **Greater security**: With your home paid off or financed creatively without traditional debt, you have a greater sense of security knowing that you own your property outright, making you less vulnerable to economic downturns or interest rate hikes.

Living mortgage-free offers profound peace of mind, knowing that you are in control of your financial destiny.

How to Buy a House Without a Mortgage: Creative Financing Strategies

2.3 Building Wealth for the Future

Homeownership without a mortgage can lead to accelerated wealth-building:

- **Appreciation of property value**: Over time, your property will likely appreciate, increasing its value. Without a mortgage, any increase in property value translates directly into wealth.
- **Equity building**: In creative financing models like lease-to-own or seller financing, a portion of your payments goes toward owning your home outright, which builds equity much faster compared to traditional financing.

By buying a home without a mortgage, you have a unique opportunity to leverage real estate to secure your financial future and build wealth.

Subsection 3: Final Tips for Continued Success in Real Estate and Financial Freedom

3.1 Maintaining Financial Discipline

While achieving a mortgage-free home is a tremendous accomplishment, continued financial discipline is essential for maintaining success:

- **Reinvest in real estate**: Consider reinvesting the funds you would have spent on mortgage payments into other properties. This can help build a strong real estate portfolio that generates passive income.
- **Diversify investments**: Expand your financial horizon by diversifying into stocks, bonds, or other asset classes. Spreading risk across multiple investments will ensure long-term financial security.

- **Monitor your expenses**: Keep your spending in check and build a budget that reflects your new financial freedom. Avoid unnecessary debt and ensure that your living expenses remain in alignment with your goals.

3.2 Expanding Your Network and Knowledge Base

Continue to build on the network you have cultivated throughout your creative financing journey:

- **Stay connected to professionals**: Real estate agents, attorneys, and financial advisors can help you navigate future transactions, ensuring that your decisions continue to align with your financial goals.
- **Engage in real estate communities**: Join forums, social media groups, and other communities where real estate investors and buyers share their experiences. This can provide invaluable insights and opportunities for collaboration.
- **Educate yourself**: The world of creative financing is constantly evolving. Attend workshops, read books, and seek out mentorship to stay informed about the latest strategies and trends in real estate and financial freedom.

3.3 Leverage the Power of Passive Income

As you acquire more properties or other assets, aim to establish streams of passive income. This could include:

- **Rental properties**: Use properties purchased through creative financing to generate rental income.
- **Real estate syndications**: Invest in larger real estate deals with others to receive dividends from commercial or residential property holdings.
- **Dividend stocks and other passive income ventures**: Expand your financial independence by generating consistent returns from non-real estate investments.

How to Buy a House Without a Mortgage: Creative Financing Strategies

By focusing on passive income, you can free yourself from the need to actively work for every dollar, allowing you to enjoy more freedom and flexibility.

Subsection 4: Taking Action: The Next Steps Toward Your Dream Home

4.1 Creating a Plan for the Future

With your homeownership journey now on a successful path, it's important to think ahead and create a plan for the future. Begin by:

- **Setting long-term financial goals**: Whether that's buying more real estate, starting a business, or achieving financial independence, it's essential to have a clear vision of your next steps.
- **Identifying new opportunities**: Stay open to exploring new creative financing options and property types that align with your goals. Whether you're looking for a vacation home, a rental property, or a commercial investment, now is the time to expand your horizons.

4.2 Taking Immediate Action

For those who haven't yet purchased their dream home, taking action is the first step toward achieving your goals. Start by:

- **Evaluating your finances**: Understand your current financial situation and determine how much you can afford to invest in a non-traditional home purchase.
- **Researching financing options**: Explore creative financing strategies that best fit your financial situation, whether it's seller financing, lease-to-own, or another method.

- **Finding a real estate professional**: Connect with professionals who are experienced in creative financing and can help guide you through the process.

4.3 Begin the Journey Toward Debt-Free Living

It's important to start the journey toward debt-free living as soon as possible. Even if homeownership is still a distant dream, adopting creative strategies today can help you secure the financial foundation necessary for tomorrow.

Conclusion

Unlocking a debt-free future through creative financing is not only achievable, but also transformative. Reflecting on your journey, embracing the benefits of mortgage-free living, and taking consistent, informed actions will help you reach your financial goals and achieve long-term success. Whether you're just beginning or already enjoying the fruits of your labor, continue to take strategic steps to build wealth, expand your financial independence, and protect your assets. By implementing the tips and strategies shared throughout this book, you can confidently move toward a brighter, debt-free future—one where you hold the keys to your dream home and financial freedom.

How to Buy a House Without a Mortgage: Creative Financing Strategies

Disclaimer

The information provided in *How to Buy a House Without a Mortgage: Creative Financing Strategies* is intended for educational purposes only. The strategies, suggestions, and examples discussed in this book are based on general principles of creative financing and real estate. While every effort has been made to ensure the accuracy and reliability of the content, the author and publisher make no representations or warranties regarding the completeness, suitability, or applicability of the information for your individual circumstances.

Real estate laws, regulations, and financial conditions vary widely by location and are subject to change. The author encourages readers to consult with licensed professionals, including real estate agents, attorneys, financial advisors, and other relevant experts, before making any decisions related to purchasing property or entering into any type of financing arrangement.

The author and publisher are not responsible for any financial loss, legal issues, or other consequences that may arise from following the advice or recommendations contained in this book. Every real estate transaction is unique, and it is essential to carefully assess your own financial situation, goals, and legal obligations.

By using the information in this book, you acknowledge that you are acting at your own risk and agree to take full responsibility for your actions. This book does not guarantee the success of any real estate transaction or creative financing strategy and should not be relied upon as a substitute for professional advice.

If you are considering purchasing a property, it is strongly recommended that you seek personalized advice from qualified professionals to ensure your approach aligns with current market conditions, local laws, and your financial goals.

Printed in Great Britain
by Amazon